O9-CFT-952

DATE DUE

DEMCO 38-296

Leslie Bassett. Photo courtesy of Leslie Bassett.

Leslie Bassett

A Bio-Bibliography

Ellen S. Johnson

Bio-Bibliographies in Music, Number 52
Donald L. Hixon, Series Adviser

Greenwood Press
Westport, Connecticut • London

Riverside Community College
'00   Library
MAY   4800 Magnolia Avenue
Riverside, CA 92506

ML 134 .B185 J6 1994

Johnson, Ellen S.

Leslie Bassett

Library of Congress Cataloging-in-Publication Data

Johnson, Ellen S.
      Leslie Bassett : a bio-bibliography / Ellen S. Johnson.
         p. cm.—(Bio-bibliographies in music, ISSN 0742-6968 ; no.
52)
      Discography: p.
      Includes indexes.
      ISBN 0-313-25851-1 (alk. paper)
      1. Bassett, Leslie, 1923- —Bibliography. I. Title.
  II. Series.
      ML134.B185J6 1994
      016.78′092—dc20   93-44461

British Library Cataloguing in Publication Data is available.

Copyright © 1994 by Ellen S. Johnson

All rights reserved. No portion of this book may be
reproduced, by any process or technique, without the
express written consent of the publisher.

Library of Congress Catalog Card Number: 93-44461
ISBN: 0-313-25851-1
ISSN: 0742-6968

First published in 1994

Greenwood Press, 88 Post Road West, Westport, CT 06881
An imprint of Greenwood Publishing Group, Inc.

Printed in the United States of America

The paper used in this book complies with the
Permanent Paper Standard issued by the National
Information Standards Organization (Z39.48-1984).

10 9 8 7 6 5 4 3 2 1

Copyright Acknowledgements

The author and publisher are grateful to the following sources for permission to reprint material:

W. E. Tucker, "The Trombone Quartet, Its Appearance and Development Throughout History; and the Trombone Quartet in Chamber Music; Early Twentieth Century." *International Trombone Association Journal*, vol. 8 (March 1980), p. 2.

Paul B. Hunt, "A Closer Look at the World Premiere of Leslie Bassett's Concerto Lirico for Trombone and Orchestra." *International Trombone Association Journal*, vol. 12, no. 3 (January 1984), pp. 30–32.

Douglas Gilman Weeks, "A Review and Evaluation of Selected Contemporary Literature for Unaccompanied Trombone." *International Trombone Association Journal*, vol. 7 (January 1979), pp. 21–22.

Gary C. Mortensen and Craig B. Parker, "The 1985 ITG Conference: A Synopsis, Final Concert." *International Trumpet Guild Journal*, vol. 10, no. 1 (September 1985), p. 46.

Keith Johnson, "Salute to Cliff, Fanfare for Five Trumpets." *International Trumpet Guild Journal*, 10th Anniversary Edition (May 1986), p. 75.

Larry Rachleff, "An Interview with Leslie Bassett." *CBDNA Journal*, College Band Directors National Association, vol. 2, no. 1 (Winter 1985), pp. 1–4; and "Colors and Contours." *CBDNA Journal*, College Band Directors National Association, vol. 2, no. 2 (Winter 1986), pp. 1–7.

Raoul Camus, "Colors and Contours." *Music Library Association Notes*, vol. 43, no. 2 (December 1980), pp. 413–14.

From John Scott, "Fantasy for Clarinet and Wind Ensemble." *The Clarinet*, (May-June 1988), p. 50; and from John Mohler, "Soliloquies for B-flat Clarinet." *The Clarinet* (Spring 1979), p. 40. Reprinted with the kind permission of *The Clarinet*, quarterly journal of the international Clarinet Society/Clarinetwork International.

Brian Ayscue, "Music for Saxophone and Piano." *The Saxophone Symposium*, North American Saxophone Alliance, VIII, no. 1 (Winter 1983), pp. 20–21.

Jeffrey Magee, "Flute, Piano Work Illuminating." *Ann Arbor News*, February 12, 1990.

Gerald Brennan, "Chestnut Brass Company Delivers a Lively, Witty Show." *Ann Arbor News*, May 15, 1989.

Richard Dyer, "Eloquent New Music—and for Free." *The Boston Globe*, November 2, 1976.

Jerome Rosen, "Trio for Violin, Clarinet, and Piano." *Music Library Association Notes*, vol. 46 (March 1990), p. 822.

Michael Steinberg, "Arts and Films, The Lively American Concert Touch." *Boston Evening Globe*, July 20, 1976, p. 27.

Michael Huebner, "Riding the Winds of Contemporary Music." *Kansas City Times*, March 13, 1983.

Chuck Twardy, "Leslie Bassett Asks—Why Is Music World Ossified?" *Lawrence Journal-World*, March 13, 1983.

John Phipps, "Echoes, Beethoven Rock Rafters." *Saginaw News*, April 28, 1985; and "Composer Entices Audience Into. . . ." *Saginaw News*, April 27, 1985.

Nic Shenk, "Music from Romantic, Contemporary Eras Provides Fine Masterworks Fare." *St. Petersburg Times*, October 31, 1984.

Jocelyn Mackey, "Echoes from an Invisible World." *Sigma Alpha Iota Quarterly: Pan Pipes* (Winter 1982), p. 15.

Leslie B. Kelley, "The Choral Music of Leslie Bassett." (Literature Forum.) *Choral Journal*, vol. 19, no. 4 (1978), pp. 16–17. Reprinted with permission of the American Choral Directors Association.

Nancy Malitz, "A Prophet with Honor." *Detroit News*, September 26, 1985. Reprinted with the permission of The Detroit News, a Gannett newspaper, copyright 1985.

Roger Dettmor, "Bassett: Echoes from an Invisible World." CRI Records, SD 429, produced by Carter Harman. *Fanfare* (March-April, 1981), pp. 68–69.

Julie Ridenour, "Style Varied, But Quality All Was High." *Grand Rapids Press*, November 19, 1988.

Richard Devinney, "Music Needs Merchandizing." *Grand Rapids Press*, May 17, 1982.

Eric Salzman, "Has the Avant-Garde Become the Establishment?" *Stereo Review*, vol. 37 (August 1976), pp. 100–101.

Leslie Bassett, "Form in Tonal Music." *Journal of Music Theory*, vol. 9, no. 2 (1965), pp. 318–19.

Richard Brooks, "Concerto da Camera." *Music Library Association Notes*, vol. 45, no. 1 (September 1988), p. 154.

Alfred W. Cochran, "Duo Concertante." *Music Library Association Notes*, vol. 46, no. 1 (September 1990), pp. 223–24.

Allen B. Skei, "Time and Beyond, for Baritone Solo, Clarinet, Violoncello, and Piano." *Music Library Association Notes*, vol. 38, no. 2 (December 1981), pp. 429–30.

James W. Henderson, "Premiere Highlights Year-end Concert at Midland." *The Saginaw News*, May 2, 1977.

Charles Rochester Young, "Some Insights Into the Compositional Process of Leslie Bassett." *The Saxophone Symposium*, North American Saxophone Alliance, vol. 15, no. 3 (Summer 1990), pp. 20–26.

Every reasonable effort has been made to trace the owners of copyright materials in this book, but in some instances this has proven impossible. The author and publisher will be glad to receive information leading to more complete acknowledgments in subsequent printings of the book and in the meantime extend their apologies for any omissions.

Contents

Tell me then that I must perish
like the flowers that I cherish
Nothing remembered of my name,
nothing remembering of my fame?
But the gardens I planted still are young,
the songs I sang will still be sung!

Huéxotzin
Prince of Texcóco

This book is dedicated to Dale M. Johnson, my husband, variously college teacher and participant in chemical processing and sales, for his persevering encouragement and, in addition, his phenomenal skill as a proofreader after I had looked at the data so long that omissions and flaws seemed to be invisible.

Preface

The man that hath no music in himself
Nor is not mov'd with concord of sweet sounds,
Is fit for treason, strategems, and spoils;
The motions of his spirit are dull as night,
And his affections dark as Erebus:
Let no such man be trusted.
              William Shakespeare, Merchant of Venice

Leslie Bassett is a 20th century composer, lecturer, university professor, and winner of many awards and honors, who has contributed most generously and importantly to the development of American music. Information derived from many sources has been organized into book form here so that his many admirers, both present and future, may find it readily available.

The biography section includes, first, a sketch of Bassett's life and career, presented in chronological order, encompassing source materials from Professor Bassett, an interview by the author with him at the 1983 Symposium of Contemporary Music, University of Kansas, Lawrence, and information from various publications which are listed in the "Bibliography" or in "Annotated Reviews of Performances and Concerts."

The second part of the biography is an evaluative description of the progression of his musical compositions during his life, divided by performance categories, in this order: (1) brass music and band and wind ensemble music, (2) chamber music, (3) choral music, (4) music for solo voice, (5) editions of older music, (6) electronic music, (7) instrumental solo, unaccompanied, (8) organ music, (9) orchestra music, (10) piano music. To give the reader a feeling for Bassett's music, illustrations of selected scores are inserted in the text to accompany the discussion.

There follows a classified list of works in alphabetical order divided into eleven categories of performance, and within each category arranged alphabetically by title. Each entry is prefaced with an identification number and provides: identification number used in this book; title; instrumentation; duration in minutes; publisher and publication date; date composed; commissions, awards and prizes; first performances and other performances, their orchestras, ensembles, conductors, location of the performance with date performed; and record number of published recordings. Compositions may be listed in more than one of the eleven categories: W1 - W6 Band and Wind Ensemble Music, W7 - W18 Brass Music, W19 - W46 Chamber Music, W47 - W65 Choral Music, W66 - W72 Music for Solo Voice, W73 - W76 Editions of Older Music, W77 - W79 Electronic Music, W80 - W83 Instrumental Solo, Unaccompanied, W84 - W93 Orchestra Music, W94 - W97 Organ Music, W98 - W103 Piano Music.

The Discography lists eighteen Bassett compositions in alphabetical order by title which appear on recordings. The names of performers and their instrument, the performing body, and the label name and number are given.

Each entry in the section, "Bibliography," is identified by an entry number prefixed by the letter "B." Annotations, including pertinent quotations, accompany the entries.

Separated from this bibliography is a section, "Annotated Reviews of Performances and Concerts," each prefixed with the letter "P." Many include quotations from the correspondents and contributors.

A series of appendices include: (A) list of Leslie Bassett's guest composer appearances from 1959 to 1990, arranged chronologically, featuring festivals, symposia, and major educational events (additional appearances at which he was honored at concerts when his compositions were performed are too abundant to enumerate), (B) publishers of scores and recordings, (C) alphabetical list of titles of his works; and (D) chronological list of works arranged by the date of their composition.

A persons index and a general index complete the book.

This bio-bibliography has evolved from my collaboration with faculty members and students as a librarian in various university research libraries in the United States where I have served.

Bassett's music may be found in libraries all over the world, and especially in major cities such as Amsterdam, Paris, London, Stockholm, Oslo, Toronto, Rome, Berlin, and Tokyo.

Such research libraries' resources can be attributed to each library's own unique community needs. There are computerized on-line catalogs connected to networks, handwritten typed or printed cards of various ages and sizes in a great variety of containers and cases, some of which are locked. In some countries the catalogs are usually for the use of staff only, and users are required to present evidence of research before using them. The most rudimentary list can be a valuable resource. Handwritten or typed notebooks were guarded carefully.

Since music is usually targeted as a specialty resulting in the documentation and collections often being physically separated from general collections, even the experienced performer, historian, or student may find that accessing the desired material quickly is frustrating.

I have written this book hoping that it may be beneficial and a time-saver.

Acknowledgments

Excerpts have been reprinted with the kind permission and the courtesy of the following publications, organizations, and free-lance writers:

Gerald Brennan, writing in the *Ann Arbor News;* Jeffrey J. Magee, writing in the *Ann Arbor News;* Brian T. Ayescue, used with the permission of the author, writing in the *Saxophone Symposium*, North American Saxophone Alliance; *Boston Globe, Choral Journal*, American Choral Directors Association; *Clarinet*, quarterly journal of the International Clarinet Society/Clarinetwork International; College Band Directors National Association *CBDNA Journal, Detroit News*, a Gannett newspaper; *Fanfare;* Instituto Mexiquense De Cultura, Casa De Cultura De Texcoco; *International Trombone Association Journal; ITG Journal*, International Trumpet Guild; Michael Huebner, writing in the *Kansas City Star; Lawrence Journal-World; Music Library Association Notes; Saginaw News; St. Petersburg Times, Stereo Review, Pan Pipes*, Sigma Alpha Iota Quarterly; Charles Young.

First, I wish to acknowledge the kind assistance of Professor Leslie Bassett in preparing this bio-bibliography.

I also acknowledge the assistance of Charles K. Warriner, University of Kansas retired Professor of Sociology, upon whose ingeniousness with personal computer programs I have relied.

Flora Silini, a dedicated friend and retired Professor of Piano at the University of Kansas, has kindly utilized her professional skills and knowledge of music in viewing this book before publication.

I also acknowledge the assistance of Margaret Oros, Geologist Emerita, Kansas Geological Survey, author and music lover, who proofread the entire book and whose recommendations have enhanced its clarity.

Abbreviations for Musical Instruments

bar	baritone
bass	bass
d bass	double bass
bssn	bassoon
c bssn	contra bassoon
cel	celesta
cello	cello, violoncello
cl	clarinet
alto cl	alto clarinet
b cl	bass clarinet
contra cl	contra clarinet
contra-b cl	contra bass clarinet
E b cl	E flat clarinet
continuo	continuo
contra	contra
drum	drum
b drum	bass drum
EH	English horn
euph	euphonium
fl	flute
alto fl	alto flute
guitar	guitar
harp	harp
hn	horn
ob	oboe
opt	optional
organ	organ
perc	percussion

picc	piccolo
pno	piano
SAA	soprano, alto, alto
SATB	soprano, alto, tenor, bass
SSAA	soprano, soprano, alto, alto
sax	saxophone
alto sax	alto saxophone
bar sax	baritone saxophone
sop sax	soprano saxophone
ten sax	tenor saxophone
solo	solo
soprano	soprano
tbn	trombone
b tbn	bass trombone
tenor	tenor
timp	timpani
tpt	trumpet
TTBB	tenor, tenor, bass, bass
tuba	tuba
vibra	vibraphone
vla	viola
vln	violin

Biography

Leslie Raymond Bassett was born January 22, 1923, on a ranch in Hanford, California, the oldest of two sons of Archibald and Vera Bassett. The family settled within a few years in Fresno and later in Madera, California. Bassett exhibited an inherent inclination toward music at an early age: "As I remember," he says, "I simply always liked to plunk out songs on the piano. As a kid, my mother began to teach me piano at the age of five or six; by seven or eight, she found other teachers with whom I studied, who came to the house." At Fresno Central Union High School he took a piano course and learned to play the trombone, his performing instrument for many years until halted by an operation on his jaw. With gentle humor, he cheerfully says, "after that I never played the trombone again." Early training included learning to play one instrument after the other, and at college he studied all of the instruments expecting to enter the profession of a public school teacher. He comments, "I have always enjoyed playing instruments. I consider instruments to be the source from which my music emerges." (B61)

After graduating from high school, he studied on a scholarship for several semesters at Fresno State University. World War II and wartime service interrupted his education and he served for thirty-eight months as a trombonist in the 13th Armored Division Band of the United States Army in California, Texas, France, and Germany. In this capacity, his early training on piano and trombone, and performance on the trombone in particular, led to arranging music for various concert and jazz bands. Under wartime conditions he remembers going to Austria and seeing the Mozart Geburtshaus in Salzburg, to

Germany where he saw Beethoven's and Richard Strauss' homes, and advancing through France occasionally noting a plaque on the wall commemorating a famous person's life. Wartime service in France and Germany ended and he returned to his studies at Fresno State where he began serious study of music composition with Arthur Bedahl and Miriam Withrow. He received a Bachelor of Arts degree in 1947 with emphasis on instrumental and choral music teaching. With the help of the G.I. Bill of Rights he pursued graduate studies at the University of Michigan, Ann Arbor, where he was the pupil of Homer Keller for one semester, followed by a lengthy period of study as a pupil of Ross Lee Finney. Bassett describes Ross Lee Finney as "the teacher to whom I owe the most." Bassett received a Masters in Music Composition from the University of Michigan in 1949 and doctorate in 1956. "All my life I was in a university," he says jokingly, "being one who never graduates from the time he is a freshman to the time he retires as a senior citizen."

While a soldier in 1945 he heard the Los Angeles Philharmonic perform Bela Bartok's *Concerto for Orchestra.* Bartok had recently died. The young Bassett immersed himself in Bartok's music and remembers being told that his music sounded like Bartok, for a time.

With his bride, Anita Denniston, a pianist, he spent 1950-51 at the École Normale de Musique, Paris, as a Fulbright Fellow, a high honor, studying under Arthur Honegger and privately with Nadia Boulanger. Boulanger was a noted teacher of composition who maintained a lifetime interest in her pupils and was an acclaimed visitor to the United States. Arthur Honegger was a member of "Les Six," a so named group of six French composers--Louis Durey, Arthur Honegger, Darius Milhaud, Germaine Tailleferre, Georges Auric and Francis Poulenc in the 1920s. In 1960, Bassett was a colleague of Roberto Gerhard, Spanish born composer, who had emigrated to England where he taught and composed. He went to the University of Michigan as a visiting professor for half a year and Bassett made himself his student. Gerhard worked with twelve-tone techniques and contributed a strong influence. Bassett also studied with Mario Davidovsky, who was born in Buenos Aires, when Davidovsky went to the University of Michigan to help set up the Electronic Music Studio and instructed students and staff in how to use the equipment. At the University of Michigan, Bassett was a colleague of Ross Lee Finney who worked with serial techniques after 1950. In the 1950s electronic music was beginning to have an impact in the United States, and in the 1960s it had appeared on university campuses throughout the country.

Following the year in Paris, 1950-1951, Bassett taught instrumental music in the Fresno Public Schools. In 1952 he joined the faculty at the University of Michigan, becoming head of the Composition Department in 1970. He was also a founder-member of the University's Electronic Studio and he directed the Rockefeller Foundation Contemporary Directions Performance Project for five years. He was named the 1984 Henry Russel Lecturer at the University of Michigan, the highest honor to be awarded a senior faculty member and the first time that the lectureship had gone to a musician or artist. The title of his lecture was "The Shape of Content." At his retirement in 1991, he was the Albert Stanley Distinguished University Professor and Chairman of the Composition Department at the University. He "retired from the faculty but not from composing."

Bassett's compositions of note from the fifties and sixties are: *Quartet for Trombones* (W14) 1949; *String Quartet, no. 1* (W40) 1950; *Six Piano Pieces* (W103) and *String Quartet, no. 2* (W41) 1951; *The Lamb* (W54) and *Sonata for Horn and Piano* (W16) 1952; *Brass Trio, Four Songs* (W8) and *Trio for Viola, Clarinet and Piano* (W44) 1953; *Quintet for Strings* (W33) and *Sonata for Trombone and Piano* (W17) 1954; *Clarinet Duets* (W21) and *Toccata* (W96) 1955; *Sonata for Viola and Piano* (W37) 1956; *Five Pieces for String Quartet* (W26), *Out of the Depths* (W60), and *Suite for Unaccompanied Trombone* (W18) 1957; *Easter Triptych* (W12), *Voluntaries* (W97) and *Woodwind Quintet* (W19) 1958; *A Ring of Emeralds* (W63), *Cantata, for City, Nation, World* (W48), *Cello Duets* (W20) and *Sonata for Violin and Piano* (W38) 1959; and *Moonrise* (W57) and *Remembrance* (W62) in 1960.

His *First String Quartet* won honorable mention in the James Phelan Competition in California. His *Second String Quartet* was awarded a prize at the Concours International pour Quators a Cordes in Brussels. His *Quartet for Trombone* and his *Sonata for Horn and Piano* both won publication awards from the National Association of Wind and Percussion Instruments. His *Five Pieces for String Quartet* won a Society for Publication of American Music Award. These achievements led to two years in Europe as the recipient of the coveted Prix de Rome, and he spent two years at the American Academy in Rome, 1961-1963.

While in Italy he composed seven major works which are still available. They are: 1961 -- *Five Movements for Orchestra* (W90), and *Mobile for piano* (W101); 1962 -- *Ecologue, Ecomium and Evocation* (W51), *Quintet for Piano and Strings* (W34), *String Quartet, no. 3* (W42), *To Music, Three Songs* (W72); 1963 -- *Variations for Orchestra* (W93). These compositions were performed by the RAI Orchestra of Rome and other chamber music ensembles. He, his wife Anita, and three small children, Noel, Wendy and Ralph, enjoyed the countryside and affiliation with the American Academy of Rome. The Rome Prize was renewed in 1962 and supplemented by research funds from the University of Michigan.

In 1964 he composed *Designs, Images and Textures* (W3) which was commissioned by the Ithaca High School Band, and *Four Statements* (W94) written for organ.

The Pulitzer Prize in Music for 1966 was conferred on Bassett for the United States premiere of *Variations for Orchestra* performed by the Philadelphia Orchestra with Eugene Ormandy as conductor. The European premiere, which was broadcast and taped, was conducted by Ferrucio Scaglia. When Bassett played this tape for James Wallace, dean of the School of Music, Wallace telephoned Ormandy, inviting him to listen to it, leading to the premiere and the prize.

Pulitzer Prizes ($3,000) are an endowment of Joseph Pulitzer, 1847-1911, publisher of *The World,* New York City, in a bequest to Columbia University, and are awarded by the president of the university on recommendation of the Pulitzer Prize Board for work done during the preceding year.

Variations for Orchestra represented the United States at the 1966 UNESCO International Rostrum of Composers in Paris. Performances by Detroit, Indianapolis, and other orchestras were followed by Radio Zurich Orchestra's recording, conducted by Jonathan Sternberg, voted one of the year's ten best recordings by the *Saturday Review.*

In 1966 Bassett received a grant from the National Council for the Arts and a sabbatical leave from teaching at the University of Michigan. This year was spent chiefly at Ann Arbor where he completed five compositions: *Elaborations,* (W100), *Music for Cello and Piano* (W28), *Notes in the Silence* (W58), *Triform* (W79), and *Nonet* (W30).

About this time Bassett wrote a manual describing the principals of modal counterpoint as they may be observed in the music of Palestrina and the *Cantiones* of Lassus, and intended for use as a reference with the music volume *Examples of Gregorian Chant and Works by Orlando Lassus, Giovani Pierluigi da Palestrina and Marc Antonio Ingregneri.* As a teacher, he suggested that students sing and discuss Gregorian chant before beginning this study. The manual includes a multitude of sixteenth-century examples of notation and their analysis. Bassett's *Manual of Sixteenth Century Counterpoint* was published by Appleton-Century-Crofts in 1967.

In the 1970s Bassett composed twenty-four works which are extant. A chronological list of the titles in the order of their composition is appended in this book.

Bassett held the Guggenheim Foundation Fellowship, 1973-1974, taking a sabbatical year from teaching, and spending this time in Montalvo, California, and Bellagio, along the lake in northern Italy. In 1974 the Walter Naumburg Foundation selected his *Sextet for Piano and Strings*, (W36), for its 1974 recording award, following the premiere by the Juilliard Quartet in Washington, D.C. For the 1976 U.S. Bicentennial, as part of a six-orchestra project funded by the National Endowment for the Arts, the Philadelphia Orchestra commissioned *Echoes from an Invisible World* (W89), which it premiered in 1976. The score received numerous excellent performances by the orchestras of Philadelphia, Chicago, New York, Cleveland, Los Angeles, Boston, and Baltimore, followed by Baltimore's recording. During these years Bassett moved persistently from a conservative position to a more radical musical image. Bassett received the Distinguished Alumnus Award from the California State University, Fresno, in 1978. *Echoes from an Invisible World*, composed in 1975, was selected by the League of Composers and the International Society for Contemporary Music to be performed representing the United States at the 1980 World Music Days in Tel Aviv, Israel.

In the 1980s, Bassett composed twenty-five works, the titles of which are given in a chronological list in Appendix D, in this book, and he appeared as guest composer at twenty-three major events in addition to appearing at numerous performances of his works elsewhere.

Bassett received another Guggenheim Fellowship in 1980-81. He was elected a member of the American Academy and Institute of Arts and Letters, 1981. He is a member of the National Advisory Board of the American Composers Alliance, the American Society of University Composers, the Michigan Scientific Club. He was Senior Fellow of the Michigan Society of Fellows, 1977-1981. He is honorary charter life member of the International Trombone Association which meets annually in various locations. Professor Bassett is involved in other professional and university societies.

Bassett received the 1980 Citation of Merit from the University of Michigan School of Music Alumni Society. The Michigan Council for the Arts chose him for its Distinguished Artist Award in 1981.

Notable in 1988: he was composer-in-residence during the month of February at the University of Southern California and the University of Redlands, California; and during the month of April, he was composer-in-residence at the Rockefeller Foundation's Center, Villa Serbelloni, Italy. At such events, Bassett enjoys the audiences who are well disposed toward contemporary music, and interchange with friends, colleagues, performers and composers.

In 1990 Bassett was guest composer for Boston's Share a Composer, which included five universities: Harvard University, North Eastern University, Boston University, University of Massachusetts, Tufts University, and Berkelee, March 12-17. He was guest composer at Baldwin-Wallace College, Berea, Ohio, April 25, 1990. Recently Bassett was awarded a commission by the Serge Koussevitzky Music Foundation, Inc. with the Detroit Symphony Orchestra for a composition played by the Detroit Symphony Orchestra on February 6, 7, 8, 9, 1992. In his letter of April 14, 1991, Bassett wrote, " The new work, titled *Concerto for Orchestra* (W86), will have five movements, of which four are now complete. This is my last term of teaching. There have been many performances and a banquet, testimonials, return of former students, etc. Very touching!"

Bassett's musical output is extensive; most of it is available. He copyrighted early manuscripts himself, but now the publishers obtain the copyrights. Scores and recordings are published by ACA Digital, Abingdon Press, Advance Recordings, American Composers Alliance, Autograph Editions, Brass Press, Franco Colombo, Inc., CPP/Belwin Inc., Composers Recordings, Inc., Crystal Records, Desto Records, Fermat Records, Galaxy Music, Golden Crest Records, Highgate Press, Hinshaw Music, Robert King, Leonarda Records, Mark Educational Records, Mel Bay, Merion Music, Inc., Musica Rara, New World Records, Open Loop Records, C. F. Peters Corp., Philharmonia Co., Prentice Hall Inc., Theo Presser Co.; Roseanne Music (Michael Lorimer), University Music Press, World Library Publications. A list of addresses is included in this book.

Extant works (some have been withdrawn by the composer) encompassing a great variety of genres provide solo performance opportunities for: carillon, cello, clarinet, flute, guitar, horn, oboe, piano, organ, saxophone, strings, trombone, trumpet, voice, and many others in combination which delight audiences. His work especially features instrumental ensembles, the usual brass, wind, and string ensembles, and those audience-appealing combinations such as a trio for violin, clarinet, piano; and a trio for viola, clarinet and piano; a brass ensemble with percussion including celesta; a woodwind quintet; secular choral music; a cantata. There are at least four sonatas -- one each for horn and piano, trombone and piano, viola and piano, and violin and piano. Church music is for solo voice, choral, and keyboard.

As might be anticipated, the duration (performing time) of Bassett's works ranges from two minutes for *Salute to Cliff,* a trumpet fanfare played by five of his former students, to twenty-eight minutes for the *Concerto for Orchestra.* About half of the pieces are under ten minutes and the remaining over that amount of time. Many, of course, contain movements which may be performed separately if a shorter work is desired.

This composer's outpourings flow freely through the years: 23 from 1949 to 1959, 23 from 1960 to 1969, 24 from 1970 to 1979, and 25 from 1980 to 1989. There are slightly under one hundred extant works. Throughout his life he has consistently exhibited versatility in the genre he chooses.

Concurrent with this versatility, his music is carefully structured. He uses conventional pitch materials, but in an original manner. His preference to voicing for instruments carries over into his vocal works where voices and instruments are combined cohesively. A religious commitment is exhibited in his work giving it a serious tone, but a happy one.

Bassett considers his music to be uniquely his own, not representative of a particular style, or school of musical thought. He finds the business of writing music fascinating when in progress, encompassed with a multiplicity of real and crucial decisions. When revising work, while crucial, the decision making is different, requiring inserts, compressing or extending, transposing, or a dozen other adjustments or enhancements to the rhythmic, melodic, or harmonic context of his work. Ideally, the next participant, the conductor who subsequently directs a performance, should be as committed to a piece as the composer.

Bassett is frequently interviewed for news articles and surveyed by researchers soliciting his opinions on the state of contemporary music. One such survey "10 Questions: 270 Answers," by Tom Everett of Harvard University, published in *Composer Magazine,* in 1980, listed the answers to ten questions by twenty-seven composers of which Bassett was one. None of the respondents had access to the answers of the other. Briefly the scholarly questions covered the composer's views of 1. their own individual techniques, 2. the academic situation for composers of today, 3. advanced computer technology, digital-to-analog technology, software, etc., 4. the role of large composer organizations in society, 5. the role of new music performing groups, 6. literary works that have influenced your thoughts, concepts, and art output, 7. experience with score copying costs, 8. dialogue between composers and performers today, 9. available sources of funding, 10. what was a recent performance, composition or recording that you found particularly special, unique and/or interesting. Needless to say, the reader finds the answers of any one composer or any one question great fun to compare with any others. The author of this book will not divulge any of Bassett's opinions here, but simply mentions this document as a reference.

Bassett has been associated with a university all of his life. His activities have been enriched by four sabbatical leaves from teaching: 1966-1967 was spent mostly in Ann Arbor and he was assisted by a grant from the National Council for the Arts; 1973-1974 was spent in Montalvo, California and April 1974, in Bellagio, Italy. He was assisted by a Guggenheim Fellowship. 1980-1981 was spent in Santa Barbara, California, again assisted by a Guggenheim Fellowship; 1987-1988 was spent in southern California and Bellagio, Italy.

In-depth study of music incumbent upon a life-time of college teaching is evident in his compositions. He teaches music theory and composition and is the author of a published manual on sixteenth-century counterpoint. All of the mnemonic devices of this art are known to him. The proliferation of terms, often so confusing to music listeners, such as anticipation and suspension, preparation versus resolution, rhythmic change, harmonic and melodic content, focal point, dissonance and consonance, are familiar language to him. Forms and styles, such as atonality, aleatory and serialism are no mystery to him.

Courses he has taught are:

Composition classes and private lessons at all levels, freshman through
    doctorate
Music of Stravinsky
Graduate and undergraduate composer seminars (on craft
    and literature)
Theory courses:
    Harmony
    Musicanship
    Solfeggio
    Form and analysis

Canon and fugue
Counterpoint for 16th and 18th centuries
Contemporary choral literature

His typical schedule features a morning composition session in his home studio followed by an afternoon at the university, where he teaches one class as well as individual students.

Concurrent with his teaching Bassett has appeared at about sixty scholarly events, giving talks to large and small groups. On these occasions, when working with performers, he has a delightful sense of humor and may offer to adjust his music to the performer's suggestions during practice sessions. Performers feel that he is pleased with their work. Geographically these appearances have been wide spread, occurring in at least twenty states: California, Colorado, Delaware, Florida, Illinois, Indiana, Iowa, Kansas, Louisiana, Maryland, Massachusetts, Michigan, Missouri, New Jersey, North Carolina, New York, Ohio, Tennessee, Texas, Wisconsin, plus Ireland and Italy, etc. A list of locations and dates appears appended in the book.

Bassett is an excellent correspondent, promptly responding to requests for information and answering my questions with exactitude. Anita Bassett has recorded and maintained an excellent record of his activities, his work, and the performances of his works when they are known to them, on 3 x 5 cards, mostly in pencil. This card file is extensive and very compact, a pseudo-diary of his composing career. Most of his works are published and available for performance and there are probably thousands of such performances hence only selected performances will be listed in this volume. He writes that there is no way to list the many contests and competitions he has judged. I observed that he is an excellent teacher, precise in his statements, courteous in the question and answer period, and generous with well justified praise, in short, the ideal professor to invite for special occasions. A list of guest-composer appearances at major events appears in this volume.

Bassett is a committed proponent for performance of the works of twentieth century composers. He suggests that American orchestras, like Swedish or French orchestras, etc., who come to America, and play their composer's music, have an obligation to carry the ball, so to speak, and do likewise, because there are hundreds of American composers, dozens of first rate quality, waiting for orchestras to play their works. Bassett says that he is fortunate in this regard. In 1983, during his sojourn in Lawrence, Kansas, at the Symposium of Contemporary Music, Bassett told this story. He was amused when a friend, who collects signatures of composers, went to a New York shop to see what they had for sale, leafed through a pack of papers, and came across one of Bassett's signatures on a note, marked with a price of $56. So, says Bassett, "if my signature is worth $56, perhaps, I should just spend my time writing signatures. Then, what is an original piece of music on paper worth?"

Bassett's Music

The discussion of Bassett's music is structured by genre for the convenience of persons studying, conducting or performing the music, for example, an instrument, an ensemble, or an orchestra.

The focus on categories is provided in this sequence: Brass music and band and wind ensembles, Chamber music, Choral music, Solo voice music, Editions of older music, Electronic music, Instrumental solo unaccompanied, Organ music, Orchestra Music, and Piano music.

Samples of scores are inserted along with the description of the music. They are *Concerto Lirico,* for trombone and orchestra; *Echoes from an Invisible World,* for orchestra; *From a Source Evolving,* for orchestra; *Illuminations for Flute and Piano,* chamber music; *Preludes for Piano,* solo piano music; *Pierrot Songs,* for solo voice; *Sextet for Piano and Strings,* chamber music; *Variations for Orchestra,* for Orchestra, and *Suite for Unaccompanied Trombone.*

BAND AND WIND ENSEMBLE MUSIC

Bassett's twenty contributions written for band and wind ensembles or for the band music repertory demonstrate his continuing strong support for artistic band interpretations, a prestigious and worthy venture. He has consistently written music for band from his first, *Quartet for Trombones,* written in 1949, to his latest, *Brass Quintet,* written in 1988.

Quartet for Trombones, one movement, is a recital piece. Wallace Tucker, in the *National Trombone Association Journal,* writes, "The composer felt his composition embodies two contrasting aspects of trombone music: the rhythm and freedon of the jazz trombonist and the sense of dignity and sonority found in the works of such masters as the Gabriellis, Schutz and Monteverdi. Interestingly, this piece does not include the idiomatic glissando, but in 1954 it was probably considered more a vernacular than a recital expression. The *Quartet for Trombones* is a very expressive work and demonstrates effective use of canonic and stretto devices." (B113)

Six works were composed in the 1950's: *Sonata for Horn and Piano* in 1952, *Brass Trio* in 1953, *Sonata for Trombone and Piano* in 1954, *Suite for Unaccompanied Trombone* in 1957. Both *Suite for Unaccompanied Trombone* and *Sonata for Trombone and Piano* are suitable for solo work for high school trombones. *Easter Triptych* and *Woodwind Quintet* were written in 1958.

Designs, Images and Textures, with its pallette of colors, arrived on the scene in 1964. *Designs, Images and Textures,* 12 minutes, was commissioned by and dedicated to the Ithaca (N.Y.) High School Band, Frank Battisti, conductor. It contains five movements for concert band, and provides parts for fifty-nine instruments suitable for a good high school band. The "instrumentalists are asked to play independently much of the time, a departure from music in which duplication of parts robs the individual of his true importance," notes the composer in the program notes in the score.

"This composition [*Designs, Images and Textures*] relates to five kinds of modern art," Bassett continues, "The first movement, entitled *Oil Painting,* opens with a brilliant, descending cascade of overlapping lines, followed by an ascending pyramid of sounds. Trills and numerous other textures and shapes appear but the movement stabilizes tonally as it progresses toward the close. The second movement, *Water Color,* opens with clusters of quiet and indistinct sounds that overlap one another. The primary figures of the movement emerge briefly and the movement ends quietly with the blurred sounds. The third movement, *Pen and Ink Drawing,* consists , as one might expect, of numerous independent lines. Gradually the number of lines diminishes and the content of the movement becomes clear. A *Mobile* provides the associative image for the fourth movement. Rustling, breathy sounds serve as background. Eventually the many-faceted central part of the piece (the mobile itself, a large metallic abstract) dominates the music, then returns to the rustling of the opening. The final movement, entitled *Bronze Sculpture,* emphasizes the brasses of the band and the shrill registers of the other instruments. Brilliant in sonority and extended in range and expressive means, this movement is the most incisive and rhythmically varied of the five."

Three were composed in the 1970's: *Duos for Two or Four Trombones* and *Music for Four Horns* in 1974, and in 1977, *Sounds, Shapes and Symbols.*

Duos for Two or Four Trombones, twelve movements, was commissioned by the International Trombone Association and first performed in Boston in 1975. The first nine movements, 1. *The Chase,* 2. *Tremoli,* 3. *Point-Counterpoint,* 4. *Doubles,* 5. *Waltz,* 6. *Rag,* 7. *Accompanied Aria,* 8. *Chorale With Pedal,* and 9. *Slow March,* are scripted for two trombones. Duos 10, 11, and 12 are double duos for four trombones: 10. *Juxtapositions,* 11. *Background - Foreground,* 12. *Mad Dash.* All twelve are short. Bassett suggests that when two trombonists perform, they tape record two of the parts in nos. 10-12, then play the remaining lines with the tape. When there are four instrumentalists, nos. 1-9 may be performed by alternating pairs.

Sounds, Shapes and Symbols, Four Movements for Band, was commissioned by the University of Michigan Symphonic Band, H. Robert Reynolds, conductor, and following its premiere was performed on its Spring Tour. The rapidly changing instrumentation featured enlivens the variable pace of this work making it enthralling to the listener. This piece was rehearsed extensively and frequently performed in the 1970s. This activity continued into the 1980s with performances widely disbursed, for example, by the Interlochen Arts Academy Band, Baylor University Wind Ensemble, University of Kentucky Wind Symphony Orchestra and Boston University Wind Ensemble. In addition many performances are being programmed in the 1990's.

In the 1980's Bassett wrote eight compositions for band and wind ensembles and for the band, in this sequence: *Concerto da Camera for Trumpet and Chamber Ensemble* in 1981, *Concerto Grosso* in 1982, *Concerto Lirico* in 1983, *Colors and Contours,* in 1984, *Lullaby for Kirsten* and *Salute to Cliff* in 1985, *Fantasy* in 1986, and *Brass Quintet* in 1988.

Concerto da Camera features three different trumpets, the traditional B-flat trumpet, a flügelhorn, and a piccolo trumpet all in B-flat. Bassett wrote the program notes in the score: "Piccolo Trumpet music (p.31,32) may be played on other small trumpets. Transposition should be made from the score's notation, written a Major Second above sounding pitch. In the performance material the Piccolo B-flat Trumpet music appears in both the Major 2nd transposition (which allows for optional performances on a regular B-flat Trumpet) and the other standard notation of a Minor Seventh below sounding pitch." Flute, clarinet in B-flat, violin, viola, cello, piano, and percussion: 5 bongos-toms, high to low, bass drum, tom-tom, 4 suspended cymbals, 4 triangles, vibraphone, glockenspiel (sounding two octaves higher) complete the instrumentation. There are three movements. Terry Sawchuk, a former student of Bassett's, trumpeter, premiered the work with the Northern Illinois University Chamber Ensemble and Donald Funes, conductor, at DeKalb, Illinois, in 1982. It was subsequently performed, by dint of its stunning musicianship, at the International Trumpet Guild, the Inter-American Music Festival, in Detroit, Eau Claire, and other places.

Paul Hunt stated: "Bassett's new work *Concerto Lirico* is a unique contribution to the trombone repertoire. The orchestral prowess wielded by the composer is one of the most impressive aspects of the work. The treatment of the solo trombone is idiomatic and the music itself is fresh and interesting. One could easily draw the impression that the solo is all legato, balled-type playing. In actuality, the solo part covers the entire range of the horn and calls for numerous lip trills, rips, and muted effects. The soloist who tackles *Concerto Lirico* must posses maturity, sensitivity, and absolute control of the instrument. It could be called a "tone poem" for trombone and orchestra, not in the romanticized, programmatic sense of the term, but in the idea that *Concerto Lirico* relies most heavily on lyric, beautiful trombone." (B57)

Gary Mortensen and Craig P. Parker wrote about the International Trumpet Guild Conference of 1985 as follows: "Following the intermission was an unannounced addition to the program, the world premiere of Leslie Bassett's *Salute to Cliff*, an unaccompanied trumpet quintet performed by David Greenhoe, Catherine Leach, Rob Roy McGregor, Jeffrey Piper, and Terry Sawchuk. Instigated by Dennis L. Horton, trumpet teacher at Central Michigan University, this commemorative fanfare is dedicated to Clifford P. Lillya, former teacher of the musicians who introduced it. Following its premiere, Lillya was called to the stage and was presented a handsome plaque with the inscription, "To Clifford P. Lillya: In recognition and thanks for his many outstanding contributions and dedication to the art of trumpet performance and teaching from his appreciative students and colleagues at the 1985 Conference in Albuquerque, New Mexico." (B78)

The College Band Directors National Association focuses on professional issues of concern to the artistic band conductor. Larry Rachleff surveyed Bassett's band involvement in an interview. Rachleff stated: "The wind band repertoire has been enhanced by very few Pulitzer prize winning composers.

Concerto Lirico

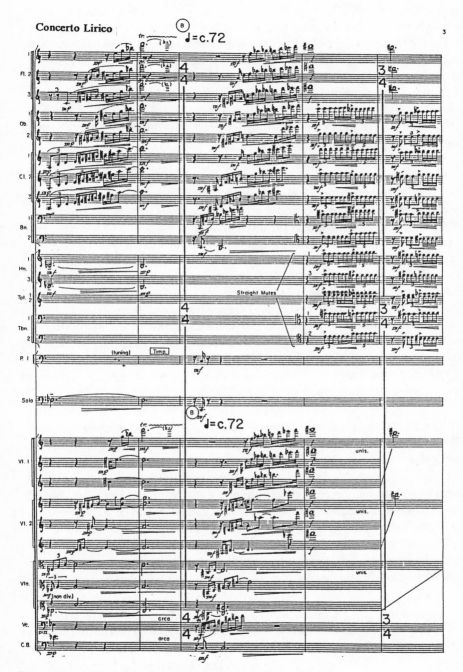

Copyright © 1984 by C. F. Peters Corporation. Used by permission.

Leslie Bassett's music is carefully structured with clear, formal schemes. The pitch material is fairly conventional, with the use of serial elements in his rhythms and short motives. His melodies can be highly expansive, with sweeping strokes of lyricism combined with a propensity for the brief, intense gesture, packed with contour and direction. His wonderful orchestration technique is enormously imaginative, with unique voices and unconventional doublings. His musical language is often very polyphonic and contrapuntal. The expressiveness and intrigue of his craft are emphasized by long fermatas, metered silences, and a variety of very slow to very fast tempi." (B91)

Colors and Contours was commissioned by the Concert Band Directors National Association to be played by bands of modest size which are less accomplished in performance and skill than many of our well-known ensembles. The Association specified that the more unusual instruments be omitted, and there be single parts for the double reeds, playable by a small band of as few as thirty-seven performers, and have certain restrictions on orchestral elements, range and solo writing. "Nevertheless, *Colors and Contours* can be played by big schools and large bands as well," says Bassett. Raoul Camus wrote, "While instrumentation is modest the technical demands on the performers are such that the work presents many challenges, combining unmetered sections with shifting meters, aleatoric phrases, exposed solos, and tutte passages requiring balanced intonation. The results are worth the effort; and Bassett has provided the means by which the more conservative and instrumentally incomplete ensembles may be introduced to contemporary styles." (B22)

A seven-page detailed analysis of Bassett's *Colors and Contours* by Larry Rachleff appeared in the *CBDNA Journal*. Rachleff illustrated his analysis with seventeen music notation examples from the score, augmented by a "Chart -- Forms: Important Unifying Elements," by Leslie Bassett. A few general comments include, " special effects are occasionally utilized but a well placed hand over bell, a stopped horn in lyric sections, or fast trills at cadential areas are welcome coloration to the textures ... finding these elements ... can generate a collaboration and communication between the composer, conductor, performer, and audience ... not a serialist, however, like many 20th century composers, his pitch imagination searches for groups of notes, both as complete and incomplete sets." (B92)

Fantasy for Clarinet and Wind Ensemble, 1988, dedicated to "his clarinet friends ... Fred Ormand, John Mohler, Elsa Ludewig-Verdehr and my former clarinetist son, Noel," was in *The Clarinet.* The reviewer, John Scott, wrote: the *Fantasy* is " a significant work for clarinet. The chosen medium, clarinet and wind ensemble, has a small body of original literature. To have any new work added to this repertory is cause enough for excitement, and to add one of quality -- now that *is* excitement. As to the solo part, it is very much in keeping with what one has come to expect from Bassett's writing for the clarinet, difficult yet idiomatic. The style is moody, rhythmic, lyrical, angry and intense. Extended technique is limited to resonance trills; the range extends to c 4." (B100)

CHAMBER MUSIC WORKS

Bassett has written twenty-six chamber music works. The following list is organized to indicate the number of required performers, beginning with duets and proceeding through trios, quartets, sextets, octet, ennead (nine performers) and with solo instrument with piano. The date is the year of composition.

(1) Duets: *Cello Duets,* 1959, *Clarinet Duets,* 1955, and *Duo-Inventions for Two Cellos,* 1988;

(2) Trios: *Trios for Violin, Clarinet and Piano,* 1980, *Trio for Viola, Clarinet and Piano,* 1953;

(3) Quartets: *Five Pieces for String Quartet,* 1957, and a *First,* 1950, *Second,* 1951, *Third,* 1962, and *Fourth String Quartet,* 1978; the first and second have been withdrawn;

(4) Quintets: *Quintet for Brass,* 1988, *Quintet for Strings,* 1954, *Quintet for Piano and Strings,* 1962;

(5) Sextets: *Pierrot Songs,* 1988, *Sextet for Piano and Strings,* 1971, *Sextet for Flutes, Clarinet and Strings,* 1979, and *Wind Music for flute, oboe, clarinet, horn, bassoon, and alto saxophone,* 1975;

(6) Octet: *Concerto da Camera,* 1981;

(7) Ennead: *Nonet for flute, oboe, clarinet, bassoon, trumpet, horn, trombone, tuba and piano,* 1967;

(8) Works for solo instrument with piano: *Music for Saxophone and Piano,* 1968, *Music for Cello and Piano,* 1966, *Illuminations for flute and piano,* 1989, *Dialogues for oboe and piano,* 1987, *Sonata for Viola and Piano,* 1956, *Sonata*

for Violin and Piano, 1959, *Sounds Remembered for violin and piano,* 1972, and *Duo Concertante,* 1984.

Bassett's composition of chamber works has been fairly steady time-wise throughout his life so far, nine in the 1950s, five in the 1960s, five in the 1970s, and seven in the 1980s.

The listener who collects sound recordings will find ten impressive renditions for chamber ensembles: (1) *Clarinet Duets* - Mark Educational Records MES 57590; (2) *Dialogues for Oboe and Piano* - Crystal Records CD 326; (3) *Duo Concertante* - ACA Digital Recordings, Atlanta CM 20003-3; (4) *Music for Cello and Piano* - Composers Recordings, Inc. CRI SD 311; (5) *Music for Saxophone and Piano* - New Directions NW 209; Open Loop Records, no.1; (6) *Quintet for Piano and Strings* - Desto Records, Inc. CRI 323; (7) *Sextet for Piano and Strings* - Composers Recordings, Inc. CRI 323; (8) *Sounds Remembered* - Desto Records, Inc. DC 7142; (9) *Trio for Viola, Clarinet and Piano* - Composers Recordings, Inc. CRI 148; (10) *Trio for Violin, Clarinet and Piano* - Leonarda Records LE 326 compact disc. Performers are identified in the Discography. Publisher's addresses are in Appendix B.

Trio for Viola, Clarinet, and Piano, (W44) is in four movements: (1) Adagio, (2) Allegretto, ma bene marcato, (3) Adagio, ma non troppo, (4) Allegro Moderato. It is a tonal work and signifies a shift in emphasis in Bassett's compositions from contrapuntal writing to chordal structures. Bassett suggests that the proximity of a colleague's viola studio increased his interest in the viola. Trios composed of clarinet, viola and piano are found historically in classical music.

The extraordinarily gifted composer continued to write chamber music in the 1960s. Five pieces are extant. *Quintet for Piano and Strings, String Quartet, no. 3,* and *Music for Cello and Piano* were written when he was a student in Italy. *Nonet* and *Music for Saxophone and Piano* were written later. These pieces vary in length from nine minutes to twenty minutes.

Music for Cello and Piano (W28) contains four parts: *Origin, Invention, Variation, and Conclusion.* The first is slow, the second very fast, the third slow with ornamentation, and the last is very slow with lively piano accompaniment. Characteristic shapes and sounds from the first movement are carried to a brief, reflective conclusion incorporating two strains from the Fresno State College Alma Mater, the College where it was first performed.

Nonet, in two movements (W30) is a showy piece, for example, the flute expanse covers the full three octaves of the instrument's capability and the piccolo softly continues on upward for a few measures in the first movement. Both movements are very fast, 120 quarter notes per minute (metronome time) and 126-132 quarter notes per minute.

Music for (Alto) Saxophone and Piano, "holds important status in the saxophone repertoire, and will continue to attract the interest and attention of large numbers of advanced saxophonists," wrote Brian Ayscue. His review is an excellent description of the music and its performance requirements. "Movement one, *Fast,* exhibits a ternary form. The saxophone's upward sweep over a stopped major second from the piano begins the work. Contrasting the opening's drive is a more rhythmically subtle mid-section, which plays on intervallic and timbral combinations, frequently over a sustained pedal tone. The music builds in dynamic and rhythmic activity, but the movement ends with a soft gesture from both instruments. The second movement, *Slow,* opens in *pianissimo* shades, and slowly gains in intensity, speed, and rhythmic complexity through a series of measures which bring the increase through clearly notated means. After a dramatic climax, the movement ends in soft tones. Movement three is a moderato which is written without bar lines. Although this might suggest quite free treatment, Bassett has indicated pulse by a series of equidistant lines, the space between which approximates one second of time, and music is notated in relationship to these pulses. The result is a placid music which explores interesting harmonic colors within the relative plasticity of the time notation. Of note are the atmospheric colors of the piano's high range. The finale is fast and rhythmetically interesting." (B8)

"Some Insights into the Compositional Process of Leslie Bassett," is the title of an interview by Charles Rochester Young while working toward a dual Doctorate of Musical Arts in Composition and Saxophone at the University of Michigan. It consists of a one-page biography, a three-page question and answer interview, two pages of selected works (Band-Wind Ensemble, Chamber Music, Unaccompanied Instrumental Solo, Music for Brass), and a selected discography. Young quotes Bassett's reply to "What inspired you to create a work for the saxophone" as follows:

"My first piece for the saxophone, *Music for the Saxophone,* was for Donald Sinta. I remember him when he was a student at Michigan and then, later, getting together with him, Warren Benson, and Frank Battisti in Ithaca, New York, after the fine premiere of one of my band pieces by the Ithaca High School Band. Don was talking about the altissimo register. He played a few notes up there and it sounded great! It was a very special thing for me and he was most interested in having some music that would ascend into that area. I wrote *Music for Saxophone* for Don. However, he didn't have it ready for performance to his satisfaction, so the piece was premiered by Libby Zinn, one of Don's former students. She played it well and Don soon was playing the piece marvelously. At that time, most performers considered it impossible, but now it has become standard literature. Don has recorded the piece on New World Records with Ellen Weckler."

"When I was working on the piece, I tried altissimo notes on various saxophonists, both here and abroad. Some could play one or two notes up there, but not others, so I would edit the piece and then try it on the next saxophonist. He would inevitably play some notes, but not others. Because of this restriction, I was forever adjusting the piece until it finally came to be as it is."

"Now everybody plays even higher notes than I asked for and they have a lot of flexibility. It was exciting, something like the birth of a new instrument. It's kind of amazing, because if you just picked up a saxophone and weren't a saxophonist, and blew into it, you might produce one of those altissimo notes first thing. Don's enthusiasm for this technique and his realization that it was an entirely new aspect of wind instrument playing were the prompters for me. It's an interesting situation, perhaps an illustration of the Bible's adage, the stone that was rejected by the builders becomes the cornerstone." (B124)

There have been many, many performances of *Music for Saxophone and Piano* through the years, and into the 1990s. Gary Louie and William Bloomquist presented it recently at the Smithsonian National Museum of Natural History in January 1990, and Bard College, Annandale-on-Hudson in May 1990.

The five chamber music works written in the 1970s again convey Bassett's flexibility in writing fresh and fascinating works for a variety of instruments.

The award winning *Sextet for Piano and Strings* is "wonderful imaginative craft at work on interesting material in it," wrote Richard Dyer. "The piece is in four movements, of which the third and fourth are particularly striking. The slow movement is very slow and very eloquent, following the witty opening movements. It begins with notes stopped by the hand inside the piano and then only slowly begins to flower into song. The last movement is full of excitingly scruffy music. And excitingly scruffy pretty accurately describes the performance too." (P11)

For the Serge Koussevitzky Music Foundation in the Library of Congress, and dedicated to the memory of Serge and Natalie Koussevitzky

S E X T E T

for Piano and Strings

(in Four Movements)

Leslie Bassett

I

Violin 1

Violin 2

Viola 1

Viola 2

'Cello

Piano

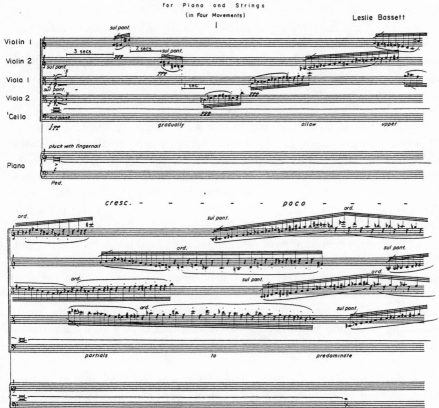

Copyright © 1975 by C. F. Peters Corporation. Used by permission.

Sounds Remembered, for violin and piano, "is an homage to Roberto Gerhard (1896-1970), the distinguished Spanish-British composer, pupil of Schoenberg, and my colleague and friend since the winter of 1960, when he first came to the U.S.A. as Guest Professor of Compositions at the University of Michigan. The sounds that have been recalled for inclusion in the score are fragments associated with several of Gerhard's late works -- a chord, a quickly-ascending line, an insistent high note, a characteristic manner of working a line, etc. As with most things that we remember, these quotations (brief as they are) are not quotations at all, for they are inaccurate. They are nevertheless, Gerhard-like in spirit, and they serve as the generative basis of the four movements. The work is, therefore, an unfolding of these key sounds, which become transformed, then return periodically to reassert themselves, as in memory," wrote Bassett in the program notes of the score. This work has been a part of many outstanding concerts widely distributed geographically and continues its popularity today. (W39)

The Fourth String Quartet was commissioned by the University of Michigan in celebration of the Music School's centennial, 1980. Bassett welcomed the opportunity to compose the quartet. The quartet "like most chamber music, is self-contained, not programmatically conceived. It creates, maintains and unfolds its own imagery and associations, reflects to some extent the language and sonorous world of music in our time, and is for me a very personal musical statement. The first of the four movements opens with a driving thrust and highly energized passages that maintain their intensity until the end. The second movement is quiet, lyrical, slow in tempo, fantasy like in design. The third juxtaposes fast, scurrying lines with ensemble chords, while the final movement is slow, sonorous music that gradually becomes fast and energetic. Several sounds, gestures and turns of phrase recur throughout the work, appearing in varying guises in each movement," wrote Bassett in the program notes in the score.

Sextet for Flutes, Clarinets, and Strings, was commissioned by Mu Phi Epsilon Sinfonia, and premiered at the University of Michigan in 1980. Mu Phi Epsilon is an honorary music fraternity with chapters on many campuses and alumni chapters in many locations.

In the 1980s Bassett wrote seven works for chamber music ensembles: *Trio for Violin, Clarinet and Piano, Concerto da Camera, Dialogues for Oboe and Piano, Duo Concertante, Duo Inventions for Two Cellos,* and *Illuminations for Flute and Piano.*

Bassett wrote *Trio for Violin, Clarinet and Piano* (W45) for the Verdehr Trio. The Trio premiered it at Notre Dame University in 1981, and has performed it, with its rich, deep tapestry, in the United States and in successful tours of Europe, Canada, Australia, the Middle East, South Africa, Singapore, Istanbul, London, China. The recording mentioned earlier features the Verdehr Trio.

The composer notes that in one respect the *Trio* might be considered a duo since the violin and clarinet usually act together with the piano as their opposing or supportive force.

"The music is impassioned, expansive, free flowing, rhapsodic perhaps but never out of control. There is a large design wherein virtually every detail can be clearly heard as a logical and necessary part of the whole. Leslie Bassett is a mainline composer. His music draws from and is enriched by the past, both recent and distant, without being subservient to it. His generally dissident language, in which movement from tension to release plays an important part, imitates functional tonality but not based on its syntax. While he has a style all his own, his use of motivic cells to generate and unify this large-scale, quasi cyclic trio suggests that he has deeply studied and learned much from the music of Beethoven," wrote Jerome Rosen in his review and description of the music. (B80)

Bassett's *Trio* begins with a dramatic assertion of the note A, stated in rapidly increasing units. A alone is followed by A plus one note, then A plus two notes, progressing to A plus seven notes. The highly energetic and forceful opening ends soon and the energy spills over into the fast and assertive second movement. Each movement picks up some aspect of the ending passage of the previous movement. The first closes with intervals, F-A and E-B, played by the clarinet and violin, and the second opens with these same intervals played by the piano. F# and C# pitches appear next in the same manner. The third movement begins quietly and lyrically, yet rises to a dramatic middle area, ending with D-flat and F, whereby the fourth begins with them. The fourth movement is placid, reflective and uncomplicated, ending with a conspicuous violin high A, the root of the violin-clarinet interval. The highly charged and energetic finale opens with the same A. Growth of phrase size, characteristic turns of phrase, and recurrent sonorities or gestures are found throughout.

Concerto da Camera (W22), shows Bassett's customary attention to detail by including a suggested seating arrangement for performance of the ensemble in the score. Richard Brooks, wrote, "Leslie Bassett attempts a synthesis of styles and techniques in his *Concerto da Camera*. The composition succeeds, because it is guided by a musical intelligence whose focus is consistently on clarity of structural design. Many passages employ techniques (such as unmetered music, resonance trills, internal piano sounds, and special muting effects) which can easily seem hackneyed. The work requires a highly disciplined sensibility to overcome its potential pitfalls, and Bassett meets the challenge in musically satisfying ways. The use of three different trumpets (traditional B-flat trumpet, flugelhorn, and piccolo trumpet) allows for some lovely timbral effects." (B19)

"*Duo Concertante* challenges the listener with its dissonant harmonic language, expansive range (tessitura), and forcefulness. It taxes the technical and interpretive abilities of both the saxophonist and pianist, providing sensitive and articulate performers with a vehicle worthy of their efforts. The challenges offered by Bassett are welcome, for this music is interesting, compelling, and of excellent quality. The saxophonist is called upon to demonstrate, as the score cautions, a mastery of the altissimo register. A significant aspect of the affect made upon the listener centers around Bassett's upper range of the instrument. From the perspective of the performer, an added complication for a successful performance is Bassett's demand that these rather slippery notes be held for extended lengths of time. While other composers have utilized this register of the saxophone as a gimmick, or as a mere affect, Bassett's *altissimo* writing is musically logical and valid. He is a skilled artisan--this music attests to it," wrote Alfred W. Cochran in *Notes*. (B26)

Duo Inventions, nine duets for two cellos, was written for daughter Wendy Bratton and friend Mary Alice Swope, who premiered it in Gainsville, Georgia, in 1989. Historically, the cello came into existence along with the violin and viola. The two oldest cellos still in existence were made between 1560 and 1570 by Andrea Amati, skillful maker of string instruments, in Cremona, Italy, so the repertory is substantial and contemporary composers have willingly carried on the fine tradition of composing for this most appealing of instruments. Rapid changes in tempo, occasionally unmetered, and leaps between octaves give the performer latitude for an expressive rendition and delightful harmonies when the timing of the notes played by both performers is unison.

Illuminations for Flute and Piano (W27), is one of the most recent of Bassett's compositions to be described in this book. It is a short essay in four movements: *Flowing, Poignant, Mysterious,* and *Fast-driving.* The work has the serious, thoughtful tone typical of Bassett's music. "Throughout there's a sense that nothing is done for dramatic or sonic effect only, that drama and climax must be earned through the patient exploration of a few musical ideas. The

ILLUMINATIONS

Music for Flute and Piano

I.

Leslie Bassett

Copyright © 1992 by C. F. Peters Corporation. Used by permission.

mysterious third movement created the most vivid impression with its rustling piano and flute figures suggesting a kind of secret dialogue in nature. The flute writing tended toward a full-bodied occasionally ornate lyricism -- not to tunefulness --that might attract flutists in search of modern literature to play. In fact, Bassett notes in the program, the piece was a response to someone who noticed a lack of music for flute and piano in his catalog. The piece avoids novel techniques -- flutter tonguing, multiphonics, percussive effects -- that have been explored in other 20th century flute pieces. At the beginning and end, however, one hears the piano's percussive sound when the fingers of one hand damp the piano strings while the other hand plays the keyboard," wrote Jeffrey Magee in 1990. (P12)

CHORAL MUSIC

Bassett has written nineteen choral pieces. The text of *The Lamb* (W54), the earliest choral piece, written in 1952, is a passage of poetry by William Blake, English artist, poet, and mystic, 1757-1827. Bassett is fond of literature with allusions to nature. The first stanza is:

> Little Lamb, who made thee?
> Dost thou know who made thee;
> Gave thee life and bid thee feed
> By the stream and o'er the mead
> Gave thee clothing of delight;
> Softest clothing, wooly, bright;
> Gave thee such a tender voice
> Making all the vales rejoice?
>   Little Lamb, who made thee?
>   Dost thou know who made thee?

In 1979 he wrote *A Ring of Emeralds* (W63) for mixed chorus and piano. It was commissioned by Ruth Draddy Memorial fund and performed at the International Choral and Folk Dance Festival in Cork, Ireland, in 1979. *A Ring of Emeralds* has five settings of Irish verse in English.

1. *Invitation*, Anonymous (1300-1350?), has the words:
   I am of Ireland and of the holy land of Ireland.
   Good sir, pray ye, for of sainte charity,
   Come and dance with me.

2. Madrigal 1. *Gone Forever Gone*, Gerald Griffin, (1803- ?) mourns:
>
> Gone forever are the hopes I cherished like the sunny dawn, in the sudden showers perished.
>
> Withered is the early flow'r, like a bright lake broken, faded like a happy hour, or Love's secret spoken.
>
> Life what a cheat art thou! on youthful fancy stealing, prodigal in promise now; a miser in fulfilling.

3. *Riddle (The Vowels),* Jonathan Swift (1667-1745) puzzles:
>
> We are little airy creatures,
> all of different voice and features,
> One of us in glass set.
> T'other you may see in tin,
> The fourth a box within.
> If the fifth you should pursue,
> It can never fly from you.

4. *The Blackbird's Song* (anon. 850 A.D.) the words written in the margin of a manuscript by a scribe when he heard the bird's song.

5. Madrigal 2. *The Red Rose,* the White Rose, John Boyle O'Reilly (1844-1900), wrote the words "A red rose whispers of passion, and a white rose breathes of love."

This completes the five settings of *A Ring of Emeralds.*

In Leslie B. Kelley's article "The Choral Music of Leslie Bassett," he surveys Bassett's choral works from 1952 - 1973. In this article, which is based on Kelley's doctoral dissertation, he says Bassett believes that "music is an expression of emotions, its syntax depends upon an initial kernel which gradually grows and unfolds ... In the early period (1952-1960) Bassett uses chordal harmonies based on triads and dissonant internals of seconds and sevenths... The middle period (1961-1966) is characterized by a change from chordal to linear style, using both styles in combination. Considerably more dissonance is used, with the augmented fourth internal being added as dissonance to the two already mentioned. Bassett uses twelve tone rows as a device in some works, but the music is not serialized. The later period, (1969-1973) is a time when avant garde such as sound clusters, electronic tape accompaniments, shouted and whispered sounds, undetermined and unmetered pitch, and constant meter are combined with more traditional practices which had been used in earlier periods. Linear writing dominates this music, and he continues using tone rows without serialization." (B64)

Four choral works of the early period are extant. *Out of the Depths* (De profundis clamavi, ad te Domine) "out of the depths have I cried unto thee, O Lord, hear my voice" (Psalm 130), is a penitential psalm frequently set to music, (W60). *Cantata for City, Nation, World,* (W48), is accompanied by organ and the singing of the congregation. *Remembrance* (W62), suitable for Memorial Day, Brotherhood, or as a general anthem, mixed chorus accompanied by organ, has a text written by Hoover Rupert ending "help me never to forget." *Moonrise* (W57), mixed chorus accompanied by violin, cello, flute, piccolo, alto flute, piano, and 2 percussion, has a text by Lawrence.

Choral works of the middle period are: *Ecologue, Ecomium, and Evocation* (text from the Bible's Song of Solomon) (W51), is accompanied by four instrumentalists playing piano, harp, bass drum, vibra harp, celesta, and cymbals. *Hear My Prayer, O Lord* (Psalm 64) (W53) with children's voices, is accompanied by organ. *Prayer for Divine Services* (in Latin) (W61), tenor, tenor, bass, bass, is accompanied by organ. *Notes in the Silence* (W58) is accompanied by piano and takes its text from Dag Hammerskjold's *Markings* translated by Lief Sjoberg and W. H. Auden from the Swedish to the English. The poetic opening lines of *Notes in the Silence* are the words of a person who is being driven toward an unknown land of steep passes and cold, sharp air, and of his being full of expectation and wondering if he will ever arrive at his unknown goal, a goal where life resounds a clear pure note in the silence.

Choral works in the later period are: *Moon Canticle* (W56) accompanied by cello and amplified speaker, embraces notated pitched sounds, and sung text, whispered, spoken, and clustered sounds. The score, in five movements, was composed during the period of preparation for the flight of Apollo II and was completed eleven days after man first set foot on the moon. *Moon Canticle* encompasses twenty-four short quotations from more than eleven master poets and focuses on five aspects of the moon and its mythology. Bassett notes, "The final movement expresses the gradual evolution over the years of the manner in which man has tended to view his satellite. From an orbed maiden with white fire laden, wandering shrine of soft yet icy flame, it becomes a ruined world, a globe burnt out, a corpse upon the road of night that has finally been violated by man. But the fascination continues."

Collect (W50), is accompanied by electronic pre-recorded tape. Bassett wrote the words to the piece after seeing a small collect used in a service for a

Peace march in Michigan during the Vietnam war. He brought the collect home, filled it out, edited it, and changed it. *Celebration in Praise of Earth* (W49), has orchestra, amplified speaker, sung and spoken text and pitched and unpitched sounds. *Of Wind and Earth* (W59), accompanied by piano, contains three songs. The first, a fragment of text, "Wind, who wanders, have you still some secret nest or tree or billow?" is from "The World's Wanderers" by English poet, Percy Shelley, 1792-1882. The second,"Earth", text by William Cullen Bryant, 1794-1878, begins thus: as the conductor's hand slowly moves from L. to R. each singer in turn enters and sustains a random pitch not already sounding. The third, "Hymn to the Earth" by Francis of Assisi, 1794-1878, Italian friar and founder of the Franciscan order, begins, "Praised be my Lord for Brother Wind."

Bassett wrote five choral pieces in the 1980's: *A Family History* (W52) with the text written by Bassett; *Lord, Who Hast Formed Me* (W55) with the anthem text by George Herbert, English divine and poet (1593-1633), accompanied by organ; and *Sing to the Lord* (Psalm 95) (W64), a hymn of praise accompanied by organ. The text of *Whoe're She Be* (W65) is by Richard Crashaw (1613-1649), a mystic, poet, lyrist, skilled in music, painting and engraving, who mysteriously died three weeks after becoming a canon. Women singers tell of a man's poetic fantasies about that ideal she. The first of six stanzas is:

> Whoe'er she be,
> That not impossible she
> That shall command my heart and me;

Bassett's latest choral piece *Almighty Eternal* (W47) written in 1989 and published in 1990 was commissioned by the University of Alabama, Huntsville, Concert Choir, conducted by Paul R. Crabb at the premiere in Huntsville on May 25, 1990. On this occasion the Choir also performed Bassett's earlier *Collect.* Bassett was present and gave an interview to Ann Marie Martin, during which Bassett said that he does anthems and sacred music once in a while although it is not a large part of his output. He is a Christian, Methodist, and believes in what he is writing, believing that it would be impossible to write a sacred piece if you weren't a believer. Bassett wrote the text. He said, " It's simply about the amazing miracle of experience and why we're here and what we do. If you had to cook up some fantasy world, this would be it, and yet we take it all for granted. That's sort of the background: we're all walking miracles." (P20)

SOLO VOICE

Bassett wrote eight works for solo voice, three in the 1950s and 1960s, three in the 1970s, and two in the late 1980s.

The three written in the 1950s are: *Four Songs* (W67) high voice and piano, was composed soon after Bassett joined the faculty of the University of Michigan. *Easter Triptych* (W66), with tenor voice was accompanied by 4 trumpets, 4 trombones, 2 baritones (euphonium), tuba, timpany, 3 percussion and celesta. *To Music, Three Songs* (W72), for soprano or tenor voice with piano accompaniment, was commissioned by the Mu Phi Epsilon Fraternity, which has chapters on many college campuses and many alumni chapters.

Time and Beyond (W71), baritone (solo voice), accompanied by clarinet, cello and piano, features the rich imagery of "Days" by Ralph Waldo Emerson, American essayist and poet, "Where was I when the world was made?" from the fourth Psalm by Mark Van Doren, and Rabindranith Tagore's "Day after day, O Lord of my life".

"Freely chromatic, the settings, which last approximately nine minutes, generally project textures of elegant transparency absent of strong tonal centers. The voice part, with occasional diminished octaves and with phrases that sometimes begin on pitches that the singer seemingly has to pull out of nowhere, is therefore wholly unsuitable for performers whose musicianship is at all shaky. Completely idiomatic, the instrumental parts make no especially notable demands upon the performers beyond normal sensitivity and rhythmic security," comments Allen B. Skei in his review on *Time and Beyond* (B105).

Love Songs (W69), soprano and piano, has three short songs as follows:

1. *Love, Like a Mountain Wind,* Anonymous, Greece; the words are:

> Love, like a mountain wind on an oak, falling upon me, shakes me leaf and bough.

2. *Tides of Love,* Walter Savage Landor (1775-1864); the words are:

> My hopes retire, my wishes as before struggle to find their resting

PIERROT SONGS
I. Wolken

Albert Giraud (Otto Hartleben)

Leslie Bassett

✦ = sounding pitches.

Copyright © 1990 by C. F. Peters Corporation. Used by permission.

place in vain;
Ebbing sea thus beats against the shore; the shore repels it;
it returns again.

3. *To My Dear and Loving Husband,* Anne Bradstreet, (1612-1672); the
words are:

If ever two were one, then surely we
If ever man were lov'd by wife, then thee;
     if ever wife was happy in a man compare with me ye
     women if you can.
I prize thy love more than whole mines of gold, or all the riches that
the earth doth hold.

Jade Garden (W68), soprano and piano, enhances 4 miniatures of Ancient
Japanese and Chinese Poetry.

Pierrot Songs (W70), soprano voice, and flute, clarinet, violin, cello, and
piano takes its text from "Pierrot Lunaire," written by Belgian poet Albert
Giraud, in 1884. The texts were translated to the German by Otto Erich
Hartleben. The songs are "Wolken" (Clouds), "Eine Bühne" (A Stage), and
"Herbst" (Autumn). These three texts are not used by Arnold Schoenberg in his
"Pierrot Lunaire," a cycle of twenty-one songs from the same source, with a
singing narrator and the same instrumentation.

EDITIONS OF OLDER MUSIC

Bassett's body of work includes four editions of Baroque chamber music;
all instrumental, written in two, three, or four parts for violin or trumpet,
trombone or bass trombone, and continuo. Older editions appeal to audiences.
Some basic historical facts on Baroque music will be included here.

Bassett wrote his first work based on an older edition in 1972. It is titled
Gio. M. Cesare: La Hieronyma (W75). Giovanni (Gian) Martino Cesare (Johann
Martin Caesar) was born in about 1590 and died in 1667. He was an Italian
cornetist and trombonist and served in various positions in Udine, Günzburg,
near Ausburg, and Munich, maintaining a fine contemporary reputation
throughout his life as a composer. His existing publications of music include a
magnificat, concerti ecclesiastici, musicali melodie per voci e instrumenti, and

three motets. His instrumental pieces contain one to six parts for cornets and trombones. La Hieronyma relates to the Byzantine liturgical rites and theories of Gabriel Hieronomachus of Constantinople.

Bassett's second performing work is titled *Biagio Marini: Sonata for 2 Bass Trombones and Continuo* (W73), was written in 1973. Biagio Marini, born in Brescia c1587 (or 1597) died in Venice in 1663 (or 1667) an early violinist and composer from an established Brescian family who received a good liberal education. He was a *bona fida* chamber music composer and perhaps the first professional violin virtuoso among composers. He served in many localities, the last seven years in Brescia and Venice. His works that survived are in printed form, the most important of which are opus 1 to 22, published in Venice, Milan, and Parma from 1617 to 1655, and these are an uncommonly high level of craftsmanship. Biagio Marini's melodic style has individual lyricism. His Opus 1 to 8 and number 22 are chiefly instrumental with some vocal parts. Opus 8 to 21 vary from one to six voices, some church-related and others da camera, outside the church. For example, opus 1 contains sinfonias, canzonas, sonatas, and dances, all for one to three violins, cornets and bass, and continuo. The distinction between sinfonia and sonata is somewhat unclear here, but points to the sonata. Marini's Opus 8, Sonata, symphonic...e ritornelli, alto instrument 1-6 parts, Venice, dedicated 1629, now shows a clear distinction between sonatas and sinfonias. Opus 22 includes Marini's boldest forays into chromaticism, his most unusual modulation and his most extended use of imitation.

Bassett again ventured into modern versions of older editions in 1979, resulting in two works that year, *Gio. Batt. Riccio: Three Canzonas* (W74), violin or trumpet, trombone and continuo, and *Daniel Speer: Sonata and Gigue* (W76). Giovanni Battista Riccio flourished in Italy between 1609 and 1621. He was a composer and instrumentalist. We know that he was appointed organist at the Venetian confraternity of S. Giovanni Evangelista in 1609, and is described as a violinist at that time. His works that we know today include three volumes of multiple works and a canzona (Venice, 1619) all containing instrumental works. Most are for 2 violins, or violin and trombone, but he scored for soprano recorder, cornet and bassoon. The canzona was an important type of instrumental music of the 16th and 17th centuries that developed from the popular chanson, leading to the development of the sonata.

Daniel Speer: Sonata and Gigue (W76), is a 7 minute work for 2 violins, trombone, and continuo, completed in 1979. Glenn Smith edited the violin and trombone scores and Bassett the continuo score. Daniel Speer, born in Breslau in 1636 and died in Göppingen in 1707, was a German composer, music theorist and author. His three autobiographical novels describe early musical wanderings in south-east Europe. As a mature musician he served in Stuttgart, Tübingen and Göppingen, Gross Bottwar, and Leonberg, near Stuttgart. During the 1680's Speer enjoyed great musical and literary activity and participated in local politics, writing a text and publishing fourteen works including music and valuable information on music conditions and practice of his time.

ELECTRONIC MUSIC

Andy Mackay's 124 page book, *Electronic Music,* Oxford, Phaidon, 1981 (B74), has an excellent description of the origin and development of electronic music in terms that the non-scientific reader can understand. It contains portraits of fifty persons who influenced its development, The Instruments, The Music, and The Musicians (inventors, composers, performers arranged alphabetically by surname). With this in hand it is easier to understand the explosion of interest in universities in electronic music in the 1960s when Bassett was professionally involved and produced three pieces of electronic music during this decade: *Collect* (W77), *Three Studies in Electronic Sound* (W78) and *Triform* (W79), which challenge conductors and performers alike.

Thaddeus Cahill produced the Telharmonium, an impractical, gigantic machine, about 1904. In the 1920s more practical devices appeared and in 1924 the Theremin, invented by a Russian scientist of that name is considered the first to attract public attention. In 1950, electronic music composition developed and pioneer composers flourished at the West German Radio studio in Cologne. When electronic music invaded the universities, Bassett was actively engaged, studying with Mario Davidovsky, founding the University of Michigan Electronic Studio, and directing the Contemporary Directions Performance Project funded by the Rockefeller Foundation at the University in Ann Arbor. (B61)

"Right now I would not do an electronic piece, remarked the man who helped found an electronic music studio at Michigan. Bassett said he had recently looked over the log of his work on the tape at the electronic studio and discovered he had spent 160 hours working on a tape that lasted about five minutes. I'm proud of that tape, I think it's a fine tape, but I can't see myself investing that kind of time. Bassett said he felt he had used up his bag of tricks on the piece. The next piece would be too similar to be exciting. Bassett noted that the novelty of electronic sound has eroded over the past 15 years.

Electronically generated sound can be heard everywhere in the society," wrote interviewer, Chuck Twardy (B114)

Collect (W77), *Three Studies in Electronic Sound* (W78), and *Triform* (W79), were composed in the 1960s.

Today, performances of entertaining background music may feature a synthesizer, played by a single musician who may be hidden behind the palms in a hotel lobby to give the illusion of a live ensemble. A live ensemble is, of course, featured where people gather to listen at fine restaurants and at social and professional gatherings. Composers, especially young composers, find composing music on electronically operated personal computers equipped with especially developed programs to be fascinating. Music heard on radio and TV is chiefly reproduced for broadcasting by electronic devices; live performances are the exception.

INSTRUMENTAL SOLO UNACCOMPANIED

Bassett has written four unaccompanied instrumental solo works: *Temperaments (five)* (W83), *A Masque of Bells* (W80), *Soliloquies* (W81), and *Suite for Unaccompanied Trombone* (W82).

Suite for Unaccompanied Trombone, written in 1957, appears on two recordings: Crystal Records S 381 performed by Roger Davenport, and on Fermat Records FLPS 49 performed by Christine Lindberg. (D14), (D15)

Bassett has a continuing interest in the trombone. He is an active Honorary Charter Life Member of the International Trombone Workshop which meets annually in various locations. The "Solo List for High School Trombonists" by the International Trombone Association Literature Committee recommends Bassett's *Suite for Unaccompanied Trombone* for grade 5 and his *Sonata for Trombone and Piano* for grade 6. (B107)

Roger Gilman Weeks' article evaluating and reviewing contemporary literature on the unaccompanied trombone stated:

"The piece is atonal with each movement growing out of ideas stated at the beginning of the movement. Rhythmically, it is a conservative work. Each movement has a meter of 4/4 which is felt throughout. There are no complex internal rhythmically structures. The full range of the trombone is utilized, from a pedal A to a D. The notes in between A and E are not used, thereby making an F attachment unnecessary. There are many wide leaps. Although there are many high notes the tessitura lies within a comfortable middle range. The difficulty in performance is due to the endurance required, rather than technique. Because there is no accompaniment, there is no time to relax the embouchure. The techniques used are conventional and there is no unusual notation." (B119)

Halsey Stevens in his review of *Suite for Unaccompanied Trombone* wrote: "The four movements of the Bassett solo maintain throughout a freely chromatic quasi-serial style which is invested, especially in the two fast movements, with a somewhat Hindemithian rhythm." (B108)

The five solos in *Temperaments* (W83), are 1. *Aggressive, Energetic,* 2. *Poignant, Lyrical,* 3. *Smooth, Yet Changing,* 4. *Singing, Nostalgic,* and 5. *Restless.* Don McKenzie summarizes his review of William Albright's *Shadows: Eight Serenades for Guitar* edited by Michael Lorimer, and of Bassett's *Temperaments, Five Solos for Guitar,* both   published in 1984, with the following statement: "While filled with adroit manipulations of pitches and rhythms worthy of the two very accomplished composers, these are works whose primary content is programmatic in the most mundane sense." (B76)

Michael Huebner, *Kansas City Times* interviewer, in conjunction with a symposium concert at the University of Kansas, wrote: "*Soliloquies* [clarinet alone] is a short almost schizophrenic work that ranged in mood from aggressive to flowing to abrasive to lyrical. The enthusiastic audience responses and the many participants in the symposium indicate that contemporary music is alive and well in this part of the country. One hopes to listen to many more new works in the region's concert series." (P21) (W81)

Soliloquies is reviewed by John Mohler who wrote:

"Without a doubt, Leslie Bassett's *Soliloquies* is destined to be regarded as one of the few really fine examples of twentieth-century writing for the clarinet, and is already considered so by those of us who have already performed it. I base these assumptions both on receptions of my own performances of *Soliloquies* by a wide range of audience types from coast to coast, as well as on my observations when hearing it performed by others. The music is at times extremely brilliant and technically demanding, at other times serenely beautiful, yet continually changing in mood and effect." (B77)

Mohler continued: "The four movement headings are highly descriptive: *I--Fast, Aggressive, Driving, Dramatic; II--Flowing, Singing; III--Fast, Abrasive, Contentious; IV--Slow, Lyrical, Expressive.* From the movement's brilliant opening roulades between F 1 and C-sharp 3 to its close on a multiphonic trill, your best, fullest multiphonic, plus trill or high B as *ossia,* the writing is excitingly dramatic. Short resonance trills (fast timbre changes) are frequently indicated, and numerous *sffz* jabs punctuate other sustained resonance trills."

Much of the music in passages from *A Masque of Bells,* a piece for carillon and dancers begun in 1980, has been re-worked into *The Preludes,* a seven movement piano solo Bassett completed in 1984.

ORGAN MUSIC

Bassett has written four solo organ works, all eminently playable. Three of these were written between 1953 and 1964 during his early years on the faculty of the University of Michigan: *Toccata, Voluntaries,* and *Four Statements,* in 1953, 1958, and 1964, respectively. The latest, *Liturgies,* six movements, was completed in 1980.

The earliest work was premiered by Mary Stubbins and the others by Marilyn Mason.

A toccata is written in free, idiomatic keyboard style, employing full chords and running passages. Bassett's *Toccata* (W96), in 4/4 time, is allegro played at c.144 per quarter note per minute (metronome time).

A voluntary is the name for an English organ piece played at a church service. Voluntaries first appeared in print in about the year 1550 and have continued with some historic adaptions to be composed and played into this century. Bassett's *Voluntaries* (W97), contains a first and secondary voluntary. The first voluntary is somewhat free, with sonority, in 4/4 time, played largo at a slow c.52 quarter notes per minute (metronome time). The second voluntary is rather fast and with brilliance, in 4/4 time, played at c.112 quarter notes per minute (metronome time).

Four Statements (W94), has no key signature, a characteristic of Bassett's music. It is written in 4/4 time, and progresses through the statements from slow c.54 quarter notes per minute, to fast c.138 quarter notes per minute, back to slow c.58 quarter notes per minute, to the last statement at c.88 quarter notes per minute.

Liturgies (W95), is best described by repeating Bassett's program notes printed in the score. "*Liturgies* was composed in 1980 for friend and colleague Marilyn Mason who gave the premiere performance on Oct. 20, 1980, at the 20th Annual Conference on Organ Music at the University of Michigan. It is both a religious and a concert work, drawing upon organ mass, toccatas and other sacred music of the past as points of departure. The first movement, a *Kyrie*, announces the rhythm of that word in its first three chords, followed by a swirl of notes and other energetic and exuberant flourishes. The *Gloria* is likewise brilliant and colorful, yet with a somewhat darker center section. The *Offertory*, gentle by contrast, opens with conspicuous high D pedal, offset during the center of the movement by solos. The fourth movement, *Trinity*, is a three-in-one canon (*trinitas in unitate*) presented in four sections. *Elevation of the Host* begins with an 8-note chord whose notes gradually rise, one by one; subsequent held-note phrases and a solo point to the final brilliant D major triad. The concluding *Benedictus-Postlude* salutes the virtuous organ music of the late 19th and early 20th centuries, as eloquently exemplified by Widor and his contemporaries."

ORCHESTRA MUSIC

Bassett wrote ten works for orchestra, three in the 1960s: *Five Movements for Orchestra*, 1961, *Variations for Orchestra*, 1963, and *Colloquy*, 1969. The four orchestral works written in the 1970s are: *Celebration in Praise of Earth*, 1970, *Forces*, 1972, *Echoes from an Invisible World*, 1974/5, and *Concerto for Two Pianos and Orchestra*, 1976. Two works were written in the 1980s: *Concerto Lirico*, for trombone and orchestra, 1983, and *From a Source Evolving*, 1985. *Concerto for Orchestra* was written in 1991.

Bassett gained familiarity with a wide range of musical instruments in his youth and writes for a range of media from solo instrument to full orchestra. He likes to tackle large orchestral pieces although these works are not requested as often as others. His concern for his audience includes the wish that listeners perceive and be moved by his music, not ignore it, go to sleep by it, eat dinner by it, or shop by it. He says he writes the most beautiful music he can.

Five Movements for Orchestra (W90), 1. Slow, 2. Fast, 3. Slow, 4. Very Fast, and 5. Very fast, but with motion, was completed in 1961, while Bassett was still in Ann Arbor, but was broadcast in Italy, by the RAI (National Radio Broadcasting) Orchestra of Rome during Bassett's stay at the American Academy of Rome. The American premiere occurred back in Ann Arbor.

Variations for Orchestra (W93) received the 1966 Pulitzer Prize following its U.S. premiere by the Philadelphia Orchestra under Eugene Ormandy. Bassett wrote: "The *Variations for Orchestra* constitute the last work composed during my two years as holder of the Prix de Rome at the American Academy in Rome, 1961-63. Begun in late November of 1962 and completed the following May, the *Variations* took shape with the sounds of the Radio Orchestra of Rome (RAI) in my ears. I attended most of the concerts of this excellent ensemble; and, knowing that it would be giving the premiere of the work (July 6, 1963 at Foro Italico, Ferrucio Scaglia conducting), I realized that I could ask for things that would be beyond the capabilities of lesser orchestras. I wanted to write a large, powerful, single-movement work that would place the listener in the midst of a form he could perceive, and yet at the same time involve him in the gradual unfolding of a thematic-motivic web that would require his most thoughtful attention. The variations are not based upon a theme. The opening motivic introduction consists of four small areas or phrases, each of which is more memorable as color or mood than as theme, and each of which serves in some respect as the source of one or more variations. The first variation, for example, grows from the short repeated notes that appear early in the introduction, the second from a quintuplet figure and other minutiae from the second phase, the third from a short but soaring clarinet line in the third phrase, etc. Naturally the early variations expose a significant amount of material that is not directly drawn from the introduction, but which I believed would be able to project and complete the sections. The later variations take up some aspects of the introduction that may have been overlooked or minimized in earlier sections. Some of the variations are attached to those that follow, or precede them, others are not. A sizeable conclusion, opening rather like the beginning, completes the work, after revealing once again several of the motivic elements in climactic context."

Colloquy (W85), was commissioned and performed by the Fresno Philharmonic, the city where Bassett attended college. It was performed during the four-day 1983 Symposium of Contemporary Music at the University of Kansas to an appreciative audience of students, faculty and visiting participants.

Celebration in Praise of the Earth (W84) (B24), takes its text from many classical sources. A sense of all encompassing nature pervades this piece as it does much of Bassett's music.

Forces (W91) features instrumental soloists, a violin, a cello, and a piano, with the orchestra.

Echoes from an Invisible World (W89) was composed for a large orchestra. Its composition was a part of a major project to celebrate the United States 1976 Bicentennial. Its was funded by the National Endowment for the Arts and initiated by six major orchestras: Philadelphia, Boston, New York, Cleveland, Chicago and Los Angeles. Each commissioned one work and performed all six. *Echoes,* composed for the Philadelphia Orchestra, was performed extensively in the United States and at the 1980 World Music Days in Tel Aviv, Israel.

The Baltimore Orchestra's recording (D6) was reviewed by Jocelyn Mackey in which she wrote: "Dr. Bassett comments that much of this music is derived from ideas implanted within the score which at first seem insignificant, such as the opening three-chord piano figure whose twelve tones recur in many guises throughout the work. The principle of unfolding and growth from small elements is basic to the work, as is the principle of return to them. This piece should appeal immediately to a large number of listeners; it is a composition which will yield new delights each time it is heard." (B75)

Roger Dettmor, reviewing the recording, wrote: "Bassett's musical diction is both coherent and unfussy; from thematic cells announced early on, he has woven a whole fabric, a tapestry if you will." (P3)

In his review of the sound recording James E. Harvey (P2) likens *Echoes from an Invisible World* to Bassett's prize-winning *Variations for Orchestra* in its flair for color and energetic feeling for putting characteristic phrases and rhythms under a variety of lights. The three-movement work is an abstract expansion of the words of Giuseppe Mazzini, leader of the 19th-century Italian Risorgimento, that music is the echo from an invisible world. He praises Bassett's command of orchestral sound and his masterful sense of proportion.

Shirley Fleming, reviewing the New York Philharmonic concert, described the music as being "notably delicate in its handling of orchestral timbres and colors, producing shimmering surfaces and transparent webs out of very small fragments of melody." (P10)

VARIATIONS

Copyright ©1966 by C. F. Peters Corporation. Used by permission.

ECHOES FROM AN INVISIBLE WORLD

THREE MOVEMENTS FOR ORCHESTRA

I

LESLIE BASSETT
(1975)

* Transposed Score: octave transpositions as usual for Piccolo, Contra Bassoon,
Glockenspiel, Xylophone, Celesta and Contra Basses

Copyright © 1976 by C. F. Peters Corporation. Used by permission.

Echoes from an Invisible World

Copyright © 1976 by C. F. Peters Corporation. Used by permission.

* Black and white key clusters covering approximately the range indicated.

Copyright ©1976 by C. F. Peters Corporation. Used by permission.

SUITE

for Unaccompanied Trombone

Leslie Bassett

I

Copyright © 1967 by Leslie Bassett.

The reader will find a lengthy list of performances by other orchestras in the "Classified List of Works."

"Throughout *Echoes from an Invisible World* there is a haunting, come-hither aural effect to the music and an enveloping warmth as the musical tones and lines rise and fall. Many of the darting, stabbing sounds appear to be random as they seemingly emerge from nowhere. The close intervals, seconds, which would normally be termed dissonances, don't sound harsh. There are distinct and diverse colors with beautiful sustained sounds, a glorious English horn solo, magnificent brass choir and lovely string melodies, all stressing a wide dynamic range and frequent, striking tempo changes," wrote Mary Nic Shenk. (P13)

John Phipps (P6), after an interview with the composer wrote: "Bassett wrote his piece in four months during 1973-74, working on it while on sabbatical in California and Italy. I sought to come closer to what I believed to be his (Mazzini's) intention, striving to evoke something of the mystery of music and inviting possible reflections by the listener upon the remarkable force and eloquence of an art which -- in spite of many illuminating studies of its physical properties and hundreds of scholarly analyses -- remains elusive, said his program notes. He used Mazzini's phrase in the title because of its lyrical quality and its perception of what the composer later called the incredible, wonderful, unknowable source -- not only of music -- but of all of man's noblest qualities."

Concerto for Two Pianos and Orchestra (W87), was recorded on Advance Recordings (D2).

James Henderson commented in a review of the *Concerto's* performance that: " The Bassett work was predictably modern but not a mere proof piece to assert the modern difference. This listener, seldom attracted to demonstrative modern expression, was very pleased with it. Bassett has found new sounds, new harmonics, new emphasis, but in none of the three movements did it appear that he was merely attempting compositional impudence. There is, as one has come to expect, a deal of startling sound, considerable use of tonic reordering, and the staccato effects so endemic to the mode. However, in this work it all moves, has purpose, relates to a distinct organizational order. It is a work which musicians must find fresh and exciting to play. It is a work which patient and unprejudiced listeners can explore, respond to, and absorb. The composer was present and came on stage to receive graciously the vigorous applause of the audience." (P18)

Concerto Lirico (W88) was written by Bassett for colleague H. Dennis Smith. Boris Nelson (P7) credits the composer with a "well crafted piece by a composer who knows his orchestration and wrote most indigenously for the solo instrument, music which was beautifully played, a lyrical voice, set against an often busy orchestral one."

"Bassett's new work, *Concerto Lirico*, is a unique contribution to the trombone repertoire. The orchestral prowess wielded by the composer is one of the most impressive aspects of the work," wrote Paul B. Hunt. (B57)

"But he never forgot his trombone days," wrote Nancy Malitz (P19). "His latest work for orchestra is a dazzling trombone concerto premiered by the Toledo Symphony and former Detroit Orchestra principal trombonist Dennis Smith. It's sort of an homage to Tommy Dorsey, Bassett explains. In fact, it's in the same key, and it all but quotes *Getting Sentimental Over You*. At the very end of the piece, the trombone puts on a whisper mute and plays the first little bit of it. I played that tune thousands of times, because we would give USO shows and they would always play little snippets of the theme songs of the various big bands, so of course I'd have to stand up and play the Tommy Dorsey Theme Song.'"

From a Source Evolving (W92) was written in memory of Bassett's father for three Michigan orchestras. This piece is in a single movement influenced by a four note chord from beginning to end, which can be perceived as three large sections, the first a varying tempo, the second slower, and the third fast. From a telephone interview to Ann Arbor, reviewer Diane Niedzwiecke quotes the 63-year old Bassett, "I compose [music] for myself, first, but I want it to be performed to great effect. The orchestra the piece is written for is second in line for consideration. If they enjoy it, they will communicate it to the audience." (P24)

A excellent review of the premier Midland performance of *From a Source Evolving* (W92), was written by critic Eric Nisula. (P16)

Julie Redenour wrote of the Grand Rapids concert. "The first [selection], *From a Source Evolving,* was by University of Michigan professor of music Leslie Bassett, who hoped for and received a definitive performance of his intriguing piece, *From a Source Evolving.* Friday night's performance of the two year old work, which was commissioned by the Midland, Saginaw, and now defunct Traverse City orchestras, was only the fourth time the work had been played in concert. This time the work received the quality treatment from the

FROM A SOURCE EVOLVING

Music for Orchestra

Leslie Bassett

Copyright © 1986 by C. F. Peters Corporation. Used by permission.

Grand Rapids Symphony which will allow the composer to take a tape of the performance to other orchestras for their consideration." (P23)

Bassett's most recent work, mentioned earlier in the biographical section of this book, *Concerto for Orchestra,* five movements, commissioned by the Serge Koussevitzky Music Foundation, Inc., with the Detroit Symphony Orchestra, was premiered by that orchestra on February 6, 7, 8, 9, 1992.

PIANO MUSIC

Bassett's works for piano include four piano solos and a concerto for two pianos and orchestra. They were composed over an expanse of many years: *Six Piano Pieces* in 1951; *Mobile* in 1961; *Elaborations* in 1966; *Concerto for Two Pianos and Orchestra* in 1976; *Preludes* in 1984; and *Configurations* in 1987.

Elaborations' four movements are: *I. Fast, II. Slow, III. Quiet, IV. Brilliant.* This very playable piece with audience pleasing runs and trills is notated with vertical dotted bar lines between the staffs to conveniently indicate repetitions in the fourth movement.

Concerto for Two Pianos and Orchestra (W98) was recorded in the American Society of University Composers Series, Advance Recordings FGR 26S.

Bassett's program notes in the score of the piano solo *Preludes* (W102) state: "The *Preludes* were composed during the summer of 1984 for Benning Dexter, a document of affection and admiration. Much of the music is a re-working of passages from *A Masque of Bells,* a piece for carillon and dancers, composed a few years earlier but never performed, nor, as a result, truly completed. Bell-like sounds flavor much of the music, with reverberation and other campanological characteristics in evidence from the beginning. The fifth prelude, for example, opens with a full course of Grandsire Doubles, a pattern popular in English change-ringing. Its permutations are listed."

PRELUDES

Flourish

Leslie Bassett

Piano

Copyright © 1988 by C. F. Peters Corporation. Used by permission.

Preludes, (seven), Flourish, Toccata, Processional, Declamation, Peal, Aria, Clangor, has been performed on many concerts by Benning Dexter and others.

Configurations' five piano pieces are: *I. Whirling Triplets, II. Lines, III. In Balance, IV. Climbing, and V. Spirals* (W99). Only the fourth piece, which is slow, contains time signatures and bar lines. The spirals (scale type configurations) in the fifth piece consist of groups of five to ten eighth notes played repeatedly eight to ten times, with crescendo in each group, fittingly apt for the title.

Classified List of Works and Performances

BAND AND WIND ENSEMBLE MUSIC W1 - W6

BRASS MUSIC W7 - W18

CHAMBER MUSIC W19 - W46

CHORAL MUSIC W47 - W65

MUSIC FOR SOLO VOICE W66 - W72

EDITIONS OF OLDER MUSIC W73 - W76

ELECTRONIC MUSIC W77 - W79

MUSIC FOR INSTRUMENTAL SOLO UNACCOMPANIED W80 - W83

MUSIC FOR ORCHESTRA W84 - W93

ORGAN MUSIC W94 - W97

PIANO MUSIC W98 - W103

BAND AND WIND ENSEMBLE MUSIC

W1   Colors and Contours
      See: B23, B77
      3 fl (1 picc), ob, bssn, 3 cl, b cl, 4 sax, 2 hn, 3 tpt, 3 tnb, euph, tuba, 3 perc,
          pno
      9 min
      Peters c1985
      1984
      Commissioned by College Band Directors National Association

      FIRST PERFORMANCE

      McNeese State University Band, David Waybright, conductor, College
          Band Directors National Association Convention. Boulder, CO.
          March 1, 1985

W2   Concerto Grosso (brass quintet with wind and perc. ens)
      See: P15
      2 tpt, hn, tbn, bass tbn, 6 fl (2 picc), 2 ob (1 EH), 10 cl, b cl, Cb cl, 2 bssn,
      (1 contra), 2 alto sax, ten sax, euph, tuba, 4 perc, cello, pno
      17 min
      Peters c1983
      1982

      FIRST PERFORMANCE

      University of Michigan Wind Ensemble, H. Robert Reynolds, conductor.
          Ann Arbor, MI. February 4, 1983. Also Alice Tully Hall, New
          York City, February 20, 1983

OTHER PERFORMANCES

Eastern Texas State University, Gary Hill, conductor. Commerce, TX. February 2, 1984.

University of Northern Colorado, Eugene Corporan, conductor. Greeley, CO. April 6, 1984

Northern Illinois University, Stephen Squires, conductor. DeKalb, IL. April 25, 1984.

University of Southern Florida Wind Ensemble, Jerry Junkin, conductor. Tampa, FL. February 26, 1985

University of Southern California Wind Ensemble, Robert Wojciak, conductor. Los Angeles, CA. October 9, 1985

Louisiana State University Wind Ensemble, Frank Wickes, conductor. Baton Rouge, LA. 41st C. Music Festival. February 27, 1986

Humboldt State University Band, Robert Flum, director. Arcato, CA. November 21, 1986

New England Conservatory Wind Ensemble, Frank Battisti, conductor. Boston, MA. March 11, 1987

W3   Designs, Images and Textures
       See: D3
       picc, 2 fl, 2 ob, cl in 4 parts, alto cl, b cl, 2 alto sax, ten sax, 4331, pno, 4 perc, euph
       12 min
       Peters c1966
       1964
       Commissioned by Ithaca High School Band

       FIRST PERFORMANCE

       Ithaca High School Band, Frank Battisti, conductor. Ithaca, NY. April 28, 1965

       RECORDING

       CRS 4214

W4   Fantasy for Clarinet and Wind Ensemble
       See: B100

5 fl, 2 ob, EH, 2 bssn, 5 cl, 2 b cl, 2 sop sax, 3 alto sax, 4 hn, 5 tpt, 3 tbn,
euph, tuba, solo cl
15 min
Peters c1987
1986

FIRST PERFORMANCE

Elsa Ludewig-Verdehr, clarinet, and University of Michigan Wind
    Ensemble, Kenneth Bloomquist, conductor, East Lansing, MI.
    December 6, 1987

OTHER PERFORMANCES

Fred Ormand, clarinet, University of Michigan Wind Ensemble, H.
    Robert Reynolds, conductor. Ann Arbor, MI. October 2, 1987
Fred Ormand, clarinet, and University of Southern California Wind
    Ensemble, Robert Wojciak, conductor. Los Angeles, CA. March
    9, 1988

W5   Lullaby for Kirsten

fl, 2 ob, 4 cl, alto cl, b cl, contra-b cl, 2 alto sax, ten sax, bar sax, 2 bssn,
4 hn, 2 tpt, 3 tbn, euph, tuba, 3 perc, harp
3 min
manuscript
1985
Commissioned by University of Michigan Band students

FIRST PERFORMANCE

University of Michigan Band, H. Robert Reynolds, conductor. Ann
    Arbor, MI. October 4, 1985

W6   Sounds, Shapes and Symbols

4 fl, 2 ob, Eb cl, 4 cl parts, alto cl, b cl, contra cl, 2 alto sax, ten sax, bar
sax, 2 bssn, 4 hn, 4 tpt, 3 tbn, euph, tuba, pno, 5 perc
12 min
Peters c1978
1977

Commissioned by University of Michigan Symphonic Band

FIRST PERFORMANCE

University of Michigan Symphonic Band, H. Robert Reynolds,
conductor. Ann Arbor, MI. March 17, 1978. Spring tour in
May, 1978

OTHER PERFORMANCES

During the 1970s there were twelve additional performances known to the
composer in Texas, Indiana, Pennsylvania, Wisconsin, North
Carolina, Connecticut, and Colorado.
Interlochen Arts Academy Band, Edward Downing, conductor, Midwest
Band and Orchestra Clinic. Chicago, IL. January 22, 1982
Baylor University Wind Ensemble, Richard Floyd, conductor. Waco, TX.
February 2, 1980
University of Kentucky Wind Symphony Orchestra, W. Harry Clarke,
conductor. Lexington, Ky. March 7, 1980
Boston University Wind Ensemble, Paul Gay, conductor. Boston, MA.
March 14, 1980
During the 1980s there were sixty-two additional performances known to
the composer in North Carolina, Texas, Florida, California,
Connecticut, New Jersey, Michigan, New York, Arizona,
Wisconsin, Ohio, Kansas, Virginia, Florida, Louisiana, Oklahoma,
Washington, D.C., Illinois, New York, Indiana, Michigan, and
Wisconsin
Many performances are being programmed in the 1990s

BRASS MUSIC

W7   Brass Quintet (Five movements)
     See: P4
     2 tpt, hn, tbn, tuba
     14 min
     Peters c1989
     1988
     Written for Chestnut Brass Company

FIRST PERFORMANCE

Chestnut Brass Company, First Presbyterian Church. Philadelphia, PA.
     Bruce Barrie, Thomas Cook, trumpets, Marian Hesse, horn, David
     Vining, trombone, Jay Krosh, tuba. March 27, 1989. There were
     eight or nine additional performances before May 13, 1989

W8   Brass Trio

     tpt, hn, tbn
     7 min
     King c1968
     1953

FIRST PERFORMANCE

Ted Evans, trumpet, Don Haas, horn, Glenn Smith, trombone. Ann
     Arbor, MI. November 15, 1953

W9   Concerto da Camera for Trumpet and Chamber Ensemble
      See: B19
      tpt, fl, cl, vln, vla, cello, pno, perc
      18 min
      Peters c1982
      1981
      Commissioned by Terry Sawchuk

      FIRST PERFORMANCE

      Terry Sawchuk, trumpet, Northern Illinois University Chamber
          Ensemble, Donald Funes, conductor. DeKalb, IL. April 8, 1982

      OTHER PERFORMANCES

      Terry Sawchuk, trumpet, Northern Illinois University Chamber
          Ensemble, International Trumpet Guild. Lexington, KY. May 27,
          1982
      New World Players, Steve Kleiman, conductor, Inter-American Music
          Festival. Washington, D.C, May 17, 1983
      Detroit Contemporary Chamber Ensemble, John Daniel, trumpet, Barrett
          Kalellis, conductor. Detroit, MI. March 8, 1987
      University of Wisconsin-Eau Claire Chamber Orchestra, Ivar Lunde,
          conductor. Eau Claire, WI. March 3, 1989

W10   Concerto Lirico for Trombone and Orchestra
      See: B57, P7
      solo tbn, 3232, 4231, 4 perc, harp, pno-cel, strings
      18 min
      Peters
      1983
      Commissioned by Toledo Symphony

      FIRST PERFORMANCE

      H. Dennis Smith, trombone, Toledo Symphony, Yuval Zaliouk,
          conductor, Toledo, OH. April, 6-7, 1984

      OTHER PERFORMANCES

      H. Dennis Smith, trombone, Peter Britt Festival, OR. August 15, 1985

H. Dennis Smith, trombone, Bakersfield Symphony, CA. November 16, 1985

W11 Duos for Two or Four Trombones (twelve)
See: B60
2 or 4 tbn
16 min
Peters c1978
1974
Commissioned by International Trombone Association

FIRST PERFORMANCE

Thomas Everett, Douglas Wauchope, trombones. Boston, MA. May 2, 1975

OTHER PERFORMANCES

Mark Andrews, Martha Taylor, trombones. University of Michigan. Ann Arbor, MI. February 18, 1979
Ronald Barron, Tom Everett, trombones. International Trombone Workshop. Nashville, TN, May 31, 1979
William Richardson, William Stanley, Joe Duchi, Stephen Anderson, trombones. International Trombone Workshop, Kalamazoo, MI. June 1990

W12 Easter Triptych (text: Bible)

tenor, 4 tpt, 4 tbn, 2 bar (euph), tuba, timp, 3 perc, cel
15 min
American Composers Alliance
1958
Commissioned by WUOM, University of Michigan, National Association of Educational Broadcasters

FIRST PERFORMANCE

Harold Haugh and Ensemble, Radio Station, WUOM Ann Arbor, MI. February 15, 1960

W13 Music for Four Horns

   4 hn
   10 min
   King
   1974

W14 Quartet for Trombones
   See: B60, B113
   4 tbn
   5 min
   King
   1949
   Publication award from National Association of Wind and Percussion
      Instructors, published by Edwin H. Morris Co.

   FIRST PERFORMANCE

   Paul Wallace, Glenn Yarberry, Charlene Symonds, Leslie Bassett,
      trombones, University of Michigan. Ann Arbor, MI. February 22,
      1949

   OTHER PERFORMANCES

   International Trombone Workshop. Nashville, TN. May 31, 1979

W15 Salute to Cliff
   See: B62, B78
   5 tpt
   2 min
   King c1985
   1985

   FIRST PERFORMANCE

   The trumpet fanfare honoring Clifford Lillya was performed by five of his
      former pupils, David Greenhoe, Catherine Leach, Rob Ray
      McGregor, Jeffrey Piper, and Terry Sawchuk, International
      Trumpet Guild. Albuquerque, NM. May 31, 1985

W16 Sonata for Horn and Piano
See: B88
hn, pno
12 min
King c1954
1952
Publication award from the National Association for Wind and
    Percussion Instructors, published by Edwin C. Morris Co.

FIRST PERFORMANCE

Ted Evans, horn, Wilbur Perry, piano. Ann Arbor, MI. May 4, 1953

OTHER PERFORMANCES

Composers Forum performance in New York, 1954

W17 Sonata for Trombone and Piano
See: B60, B107
tbn, pno
10 min
King c1954, c1967,
1954

FIRST PERFORMANCE

Leslie and Anita Bassett. Ann Arbor, MI. April 23, 1954

OTHER PERFORMANCES

University of Wisconsin. Eau Claire, WI. March 7, 1979
University of Michigan. Ann Arbor, MI. March 18, 1979
Nashville International Trombone Workshop. Nashville, TN. May 1979

W18 Suite for Unaccompanied Trombone
See: B60, B108, B119, D14, D15
2 or 4 tbn
6 min
Philharmonia Music c1967, Peters c1969
1957

FIRST PERFORMANCE

Roger Davenport, trombone. Decatur, IA. May 27, 1964

OTHER PERFORMANCES

Peter Vivona, trombone, Northern Arizona University. Falstaff, AZ.
    November 24, 1985
L. Campbell, trombone, Louisiana State University. Baton Rouge, LA.
    1979
Thomas Olcott, trombone, Juilliard School of Music. New York, NY.
    1979
Buddy Baker, International Trombone Workshop. Nashville, TN. 1979

RECORDINGS

Crystal S 381
Fermat FLPS 49

CHAMBER MUSIC

W19　Woodwind Quintet

　　　fl, ob, cl, hn, bssn
　　　11 min
　　　American Composers Alliance
　　　1958

　　　FIRST PERFORMANCE

　　　University of Michigan, Wood Wind Quintet. Ann Arbor, MI. July 16,
　　　　　1958

W20　Cello Duets

　　　cello
　　　10 min
　　　American Composers Alliance
　　　1959

　　　FIRST PERFORMANCE

　　　Norman Fischer, Harold Cruthirds. Interlochen, MI. November
　　　　　13, 1966

W21　Clarinet Duets
　　　See: D1
　　　cl
　　　10 min

University Music C1977
1955

FIRST PERFORMANCE

John Mohler, clarinet, John Bauer, clarinet. Ann Arbor, MI. April 26,
1956

RECORDING

Mark MES 57590

W22   Concerto da Camera for Trumpet and Chamber Ensemble
See: B19
tpt, fl, cl, vln, vla, cello, pno, perc
18 min
Peters c1982
1981
Commissioned for Terry Sawchuk

FIRST PERFORMANCE

Terry Sawchuk, trumpet, Northern Illinois University Chamber
Ensemble, Donald Funes, conductor. DeKalb, IL. April 8, 1982

OTHER PERFORMANCES

Terry Sawchuk, trumpet, Northern Illinois University Chamber
Ensemble, International Trumpet Guild. Lexington, KY. May 27,
1982
New World Players, Steve Kleiman, conductor, Inter-American Music
Festival. Washington, D.C. May 17, 1983
Detroit Contemporary Chamber Ensemble, John Daniel, trumpet, Barrett
Kalellis, conductor. Detroit, MI. March 8, 1987
University of Wisconsin-Eau Claire Chamber Orchestra, Ivar Lunde,
conductor. Eau Claire, WI. March 3, 1989

W23   Dialogues
See: D4
ob, pno

14 min
Peters c1990
1987
Commissioned by Barry Kroeker of Penn State University

FIRST PERFORMANCE

Barry Kroeker, oboe, Stephen Smith, piano. Penn State
     University. University Park, PA. April 6, 1988

RECORDING

Crystal CD 326

W24 Duo Concertante
     See: B27, D5
     alto sax, pno
     15 min
     Peters c1988
     1984
     Commissioned by Concert Artists Guild of New York with funds from
          Tcherepnin Society and public funds from the New York State
          Council on the Arts for 1984

FIRST PERFORMANCE

Concert Artists Guild Award winner, Stephen Jordheim; Carnegie Recital
     Hall, Stephen Jordheim, alto saxophone, Ted Rehl, piano. New
     York City. May 21, 1985

RECORDING

ACA Digital, Atlanta CM 20003-3

W25 Duo-Inventions (nine duets)

     2 cello
     15 min
     Peters c 1990
     1988

Written for Wendy Bratton and Mary Alice Swope

FIRST PERFORMANCE

Wendy Bratton, cello, Mary Alice Swope, cello. Gainesville, GA.
    February 3, 1989

W26 Five Pieces for String Quartet

2 vl, vla, cello
8 min
Highgate (Galaxy) c1960
1957
Society for Publication of Music Award, 1960

FIRST PERFORMANCE

Stanley Quartet. Ann Arbor, MI. July 29, 1958

W27 Illuminations for Flute and Piano
     See: B111, P12
     fl, pno
     12 min
     Peters c1990
     1989
     Written for Bryan Keys Duo

FIRST PERFORMANCE

Bryan Keys Duo, Keith Bryan, flute, Karen Keys, piano University
    Musical Society Faculty Artists Concert. Ann Arbor, MI. February
    11, 1990

W28 Music for Cello and Piano
     See: D7
     cello, pno
     11 min
     Peters c1971
     1966

FIRST PERFORMANCE

Fred Dempster, cello, Bob Bennett, piano. California State University. Fresno, CA. November 20, 1966

OTHER PERFORMANCES

Orchestra Hall, Detroit, MI. January 14, 1979

RECORDING

CRI 311

W29   Music for Saxophone and Piano
      See: B8, B79, B106, D8, D9, P22
      alto sax, pno
      11 min
      Peters c1969
      1968

FIRST PERFORMANCE

Elizabeth Zinn, alto saxophone, Daniel Durand. Tempe, AZ. August 1, 1968

OTHER PERFORMANCES

Michael Nascimben, saxophone, Rhonda Bartsch, piano, University of Michigan. Ann Arbor, MI. July 8, 1969
Max Plank, saxophone, Elaine Jacobsen, piano, Eastern Michigan University, Ypsilante, MI. March 1, 1970, and February 22, 1971
During 1971 more performances were given in Michigan and California
Gary Grey, saxophone, Irma Vallecillo, piano, University of California, Los Angeles. February 9, 1972
Susan Nelson, saxophone, Robert Gates, piano. Amerika Haus, Vienna. March 7, 1972
Susan Nelson, saxophone, Ginger Reynolds, piano, National Music Congress. Interlochen, MI. August 17, 1972
Don Sinta, saxophone, International Saxophone Congress. Toronto, Canada. August 25, 1972. Also performed at the Music Educators National Conference, and Palomar College, San Marcos, CA, 1973

Barry Kernfeld, saxophone, University of California, Davis, June 4,1974

During 1975 through 1979, performances were given in Ohio, Wisconsin, Illinois, Maryland, California, Texas, as well as Michigan

Eugene Rousseau, saxophone, Hans Graf, piano, Hochschule fur Musik. Vienna, Austria. October 28, 1981

During 1981 through 1985, additional performances were given in New York City, Tennessee, Michigan, Ohio, and Pennsylvania

Dale Wolford, saxophone, Ivan Rosenbloom, Composers Inc., Veterans War Memorial, Van Ness Ave., San Francisco, CA. April 28, 1987

Bassett Festival, Crane School of Music, Potsdam College, SUNY. February 7, 1989

Gary Louie, saxophone, William Bloomquist, piano, Smithsonian National Museum of Natural History, Washington, D.C. January 21, 1990

Bard College, Annandale-on-Hudson, NY. May 17, 1990

RECORDINGS

New World NW 209
Open Loop no.1

W30   Nonet
See: P21
fl, ob, cl, bssn, tpt, hn, tbn, tuba, pno
9 min
Peters c1969
1967
Commissioned by Ithaca College

FIRST PERFORMANCE

Ithaca College, Gregg Smith, conductor. Ithaca, NY. April 16, 1968

OTHER PERFORMANCES

New Music Ensemble, David Stock, conductor. Pittsburgh, PA. November 19, 1978

1983 Symposium of Contemporary Music, University of Kansas. John Boulton, flute and piccolo; Susan Hicks, oboe; Lawrence Maxey, clarinet; Alan Hoskins, bassoon; Thomas Bontrager, trumpet;

David Bushouse, horn; Stephan Anderson, trombone; Scott
Watson, tuba; Richard Reber, piano; Charles Hoag, conductor.
Lawrence, KS. March 8, 1983.

W31 Pierrot Songs (Text: Albert Giraud, translated into German by O.E.
Hartleben)

soprano (voice), fl, cl, vln, cello, pno
12 min
Peters c1989
1988
Commissioned by Schoenberg Institute, University of Southern
California, Los Angeles, CA

FIRST PERFORMANCE

First song premiered by Christine Schadeberg, soprano, and New York
New Music Ensemble, Robert Black, conductor. Bing Theater,
Museum of Art. Los Angeles, CA. November 7, 1988. Also at
Pomona College, Claremont, CA. November 12, 1988, and Merkin
Concert Hall, New York City. November 21, 1980
Second and third songs premiered by Lucy Shelton, soprano, and Da
Capo Chamber Players. University of Southern California, Los
Angeles, CA. January 25, 1989

OTHER PERFORMANCES

Laura Lamport, and Contemporary Directors Ensemble, Richard
Rosenberg, conductor. University of Michigan, Ann Arbor, MI.
February 15, 1989

Note: Has texts not used by Schoenberg in his "Pierrot Lunaire"

W32 Quintet, Brass
See: P4
2 tpt, hn, tbn, tuba
14 min
Peters c1989
1988

FIRST PERFORMANCE

Chestnut Brass Company, First Presbyterian Church, Philadelphia, PA.
  Bruce Barrie, Thomas Cook, trumpets, Marian Hesse, horn, David
  Vining, trombone, Jay Krosh, tuba. March 27, 1989. There were
  eight or nine additional performances before May 13, 1989

W33 Quintet for Strings

  2 vln, vla, cello, d bass
  18 min
  American Composers Alliance
  1954

  FIRST PERFORMANCE

  Stanley Quartet, Clyde Thompson. Ann Arbor, MI. December 5, 1955

W34 Quintet for Piano and Strings
  See: D10
  2 vln, vla, cello, pno
  20 min
  American Composers Alliance
  1962

  FIRST PERFORMANCE

  Societa Cammeristica Italiana. Rome, Italy. June 10,1962

W35 Sextet for Flutes, Clarinets, and Strings
  See: P14
  fl, alto fl, cl, b cl, cello, d bass
  14 min
  Peters c1982
  1979
  Commissioned by Mu Phi Epsilon Sinfonia

  FIRST PERFORMANCE

  Contemporary Directions Ensemble, University of Michigan, Stephen
    Osmond, conductor. Ann Arbor, MI. February 23, 1980

W36 Sextet for Piano and Strings
     See: B101, D11, P1
     pno, 2 vln, 2 vla, cello
     19 min
     American Composers Alliance, Peters c 1975
     1971
     Commissioned by Koussevitsky Foundation in the Library of Congress
          Walter W. Naumburg Foundation Recording Prize

FIRST PERFORMANCE

Juilliard Quartet, (Robert Mann, Earl Carlyss, Samuel Rhodes, Claus
     Adam), John Graham, viola, William Masselos, piano, Coolidge
     Auditorium, Library of Congress. Washington, D.C. April 27-8,
     1972. The program of the 28th was broadcast.

OTHER PERFORMANCES

Concord String Quartet, (Mark Sokol, Andrew Jennings, John
     Kochinowski, Norman Fischer), John Graham viola, Gilbert
     Kalisch, piano. This performance is on a recording.
Harvard Chamber Players, Richard Kogan, piano. Harvard University,
     Cambridge, MA. July 19, 1976
Pro Arte Quartet, Norman Paulu, Martha Francis Blum, Richard Blum,
     Harry Karp, with David Becker, viola, and Todd Wellbourne,
     piano. University of Wisconsin, Madison, WI. November 9, 1984.
     Also at Lawrence University, Appleton, WI. November 19, 1984.
     Also at Madison, WI, and for broadcast "Live from the Elvahjem"
     December 2, 1984

RECORDING

CRI 323

W37 Sonata for Viola and Piano

vla, pno
18 min
American Composers Alliance c1957
1956

FIRST PERFORMANCE

Robert and Lydia Courte. Ann Arbor, MI. December 13, 1957

W38   Sonata for Violin and Piano

vln, pno
16 min
American Composers Alliance

FIRST PERFORMANCE

Gustave Rosseels, Benning Dexter. Ann Arbor, MI. November 17, 1960

W39 Sounds Remembered
      See: D13
      vln, pno
      17 min
      American Composers Alliance, Peters c1975
      1972
      Commissioned by McKim Foundation, Library of Congress

FIRST PERFORMANCE

Charles Treger, violin, Samuel Sanders, piano, Coolidge Auditorium,
      Library of Congress. Washington, D.C. December 8, 1972.
      Recorded the next morning for Desto Records

OTHER PERFORMANCES

Angel Reyes, violin, Paul Boylan, piano, University of Michigan, Ann
      Arbor, MI. Contemporary Music Festival. November 2, 1973
Lauren Jackey, violin, Doris Meierotto, piano. Saratoga, CA. March 9,
      1974. Also California State University, San Jose, CA. May 9, 1974

Angel Reyes, violin, Paul Boylan, piano, National Music Camp,
   Interlochen, MI. July 12, 1974

Alfio Pignatti, violin, Dady Mehta, piano, Eastern Michigan University,
   Ypsilanti, MI. October 10, 1977

Max Huls, violin, John Boatner, piano, Memphis State University,
   Memphis, TN. February 27, 1982

Karen Clarke Riordan, violin, Carolyn Bridges, piano, Florida State
   University, Tallahassee, FL. New Music Festival. February 26,
   1983

Julius Heggi, violin, Charlotte Heggi, piano, Williams College,
   Williamstown, MA. April 3, 1983

Naoka Tanaka, violin, Dina Koston, piano. Theater Chamber Players of
   Kennedy Center, Coolidge Auditorium, Library of Congress.
   Washington, D.C., February 13, 1987. McKim Fund

RECORDING

Desto DC 7142

W40   String Quartet, no. 1

Honorable mention, James Phelan Competition, CA, 1950

FIRST PERFORMANCE

Larry Owen, Andy Lisko, Edw. Troupin, Joan Bullen Lewis. Ann Arbor,
   MI. February 22, 1950

W41   String Quartet, no. 2

Prize awarded at Concours International pour Quators a Cordes, Brussels

FIRST PERFORMANCE

A quartet in Paris, names not available, June 10, 1951, while Bassett was
   a Fulbright composer at the Ecole Normale de Musique. A student
   work, now withdrawn

W42   String Quartet, no. 3

 2 vln, vla, cello
 18 min
 American Composers Alliance
 1962

 FIRST PERFORMANCE

 American Quartet. Rome, Italy. May 22, 1963

W43   String Quartet, no.4

 2 vln, vla, cello
 21 min
 Merion, Presser c1980
 1978
 A Centennial Commission by the School of Music, University of
     Michigan

 FIRST PERFORMANCE

 New World String Quartet. Ann Arbor, MI. March 26, 1980

W44   Trio for Viola, Clarinet and Piano
 See: D16
 vla, cl, pno
 14 min
 American Composers Alliance, Peters c1980
 1953

 FIRST PERFORMANCE

 David Ireland, viola, William Stubbins, clarinet, Mary Stubbins, piano.
     Ann Arbor, MI. November 15, 1953

 RECORDING

 CRI 148

W45   Trio for Violin, Clarinet and Piano
      See: B95, B112, D17
      vln, cl, pno
      17 min
      Peters c1987
      1980
      Commissioned by Verdehr Trio with funds from Michigan Council for the
          Arts

FIRST PERFORMANCE

Verdehr Trio, Walter Verdehr, violin, Elsa Ludewig-Verdehr, clarinet,
Gary Kirkpatrich, piano, Notre Dame University. Notre Dame,
IN. October 6, 1981. Also William Patterson College, NJ. October 15,
1981. Tour of Germany: Karl-Friederich Schule, Emmerdinger (near
Freiburg), October 17, 1981, Concert Hall of Ernst von   Hulsen-Haus,
Marburg, October 31, 1981, Nordwestdeutsche Musikakademie, Detmold,
November 1, 1981, Austrian Society for Music, Vienna. November 10,
1981.

OTHER PERFORMANCES

In 1982 the Verdehr Trio performed this work in Oregon, Canada, eight
      performances in Australia, Singapore, Istanbul, London, Detroit
      and New York
In 1983 and 1984, this work was performed at Cornell University, Ithaca,
      NY, at the International Clarinet Congress in Denver, and for the
      College Music Society in Michigan at a Bassett Concert in Ohio
In 1984 the Verdehr Trio performed it on its tour of Europe, Middle East,
      South Asia, and at the Central, the Xi'an, and Shanghai
      Conservatories in China
In 1985 it was performed by the Verdehr Trio at the Contemporary Music
      Symposium in Lawrence, Kansas, and in Michigan at East Lansing,
      and Midland Center for the Arts, Midland, MI
Henry Zielinski, violin, Robert Riseling, clarinet, Marion Miller-
      Wasse, piano, University of Western Ontario. London, Canada.
      January 23, 1987, Verdehr Trio broadcast, WKAR TV Lansing,
      MI. March 8, 1987, and performed April 29, 1988 at the University
      of Kansas, Lawrence, KS, for the American Society of Composers,
      Inc.

RECORDING

Leonarda LE 326 compact disc

W46 Wind Music

fl, ob, cl, hn, bssn, alto sax
11 min
Merion, Presser c1977
1975
Commissioned by University of Wisconsin-River Falls

FIRST PERFORMANCE

University of Wisconsin-River Falls, Robert Samarotto, conductor. River
    Falls, WI. May 5, 1976

OTHER PERFORMANCES

Contemporary Music Ensemble, Northwestern University, William
    Karlins, conductor. Evanston, IL. April 25, 1979

CHORAL MUSIC

W47 Almighty Eternal
     See: P20
     SATB
     6 MIN
     Peters c1990
     1989
     Commissioned by University of Alabama

     FIRST PERFORMANCE

     Choir of University of Alabama, R. Paul Crabb, conductor. Huntsville,
          AL. May 25, 1990

W48 Cantata, for City, Nation, World (texts: hymns, others)

     SABT, optional, children's choir, tenor, 4 tbn, organ,
     congregation
     11 min
     American Composers Alliance
     1959
     Commissioned by Three-Choir Fest, Buffalo, NY

     FIRST PERFORMANCE

     Three-Choir Fest, Hans Vigeland, conductor. Buffalo, NY. February 21,
          1960

W49 Celebration in Praise of Earth (texts: assorted environmental texts)
      See: B23, B24, B25
      SATB, amplified speaker, 2 fl (piccs), ob, EH, 2 cl, 2 bssn, 3 hn, 2 tpt, 2
      tbn, tuba, pno-cel, harp, 4 perc, strings
      13 min
      Peters c1971
      1970
      Commissioned by Baldwin-Wallace College for its centennial

      FIRST PERFORMANCE

      Baldwin-Wallace College, George Poinar, conductor. Berea, OH. October
            14, 1971

W50 Collect (text: Leslie Bassett)
      See: P20
      SATB, electronic tape
      5 min
      World Library c1970
      1969
      Commissioned by Upsala College

      FIRST PERFORMANCE

      Upsala College Choir, Richard Toensing, conductor. East Orange, NJ.
            March 23,1969

      OTHER PERFORMANCES

      Santa Clara Chorale, Lynn Sutleff, conductor. Santa Clara, CA. June 3,
            1979
      1983 Symposium of Contemporary Music, University of Kansas, James
            Ralston, conductor. March 1983

W51 Ecologue, Ecomium and Evocation (text: Song of Songs)

      SAA, 4 instrumentalists playing pno, harp, b dr, vibra, cel, cymbals
      11 min
      American Composers Alliance
      1962

FIRST PERFORMANCE

Eastern Michigan University, Emily Lowe, conductor. Ypsilanti, MI.
    January 13, 1966

W52 A Family History (text: Leslie Bassett)

SATB, pno
4 min
1981

W53 Hear My Prayer, O Lord (text: Psalm 64)
See: B121
children (SA), organ
3 min
Peters c1967
1965

FIRST PERFORMANCE

Childrens' Choir First Methodist Church. Elizabeth Katz, conductor. Ann
    Arbor, MI. November 13, 1966

W54 Lamb (text: William Blake)

SATB, pno
3 min
American Composers Alliance
1952

FIRST PERFORMANCE

Michigan Singers, Maynard Klein, conductor. Ann Arbor, MI. November
    16, 1952

W55 Lord, Who Hast Formed Me (anthem text: George Herbert)

SATB, organ (piano)
3 min
Peters c1987
1981

FIRST PERFORMANCE

Chancel Choir, First United Methodist Church. Ann Arbor, MI. Emily
Lowe, conductor. March 14, 1982

OTHER PERFORMANCES

University of Michigan Chamber Choir, Theo Morrison, conductor. Ann
Arbor, MI. October 21, 1988

W56 Moon Canticle (text from numerous sources about the moon)

SATB, cello, amplified speaker
17 min
Peters c1971
1969
Commissioned by New York State Music Association

FIRST PERFORMANCE

New York All-State Choir, Thomas Hilbish, conductor. Concord Hotel,
New York, NY. December 10, 1969

W57 Moonrise (text: D. H. Lawrence)

SAA, vln, 2 vla, cello, fl, picc, alto fl, pno, 2 perc
7 min
American Composers Alliance
1960
Commissioned by Wayne State University

FIRST PERFORMANCE

Wayne State University Womens Chorus, Malcolm Johns, conductor.
Detroit, MI. May 6, 1960

W58 Notes in the Silence (text: Dag Hammerskjold)

SATB, pno
9 min
Peters c1973

1966

FIRST PERFORMANCE

University of Michigan Chamber Choir, Thomas Hilbish, conductor. Ann
Arbor, MI. January 22, 1967

W59 Of Wind and Earth (text: Percy Bysshe Shelley, William Cullen Bryant,
Francis of Assisi, Saint)

SATB, pno
9 min
Peters c1978
1973
Commissioned by Ohio Music Education Association

FIRST PERFORMANCE

Ohio Music Education Association, Ronald Hill, conductor. Columbus,
OH. February 8, 1974

OTHER PERFORMANCES

University of Michigan Chamber Choir, Thomas Hilbish, conductor.
Performed on the tour of Eastern Europe
1983 Symposium of Contemporary Music, University of Kansas, James
Ralston, conductor. Lawrence, KS. March 1983

W60 Out of the Depths (de Profundis, Psalm 130)

SATB, organ
4 min
American Composers Alliance
1957

FIRST PERFORMANCE

Methodist Church, Ann Arbor, MI, Lester McCoy, Conductor. February
9, 1958

W61 Prayers for Divine Service (in Latin)

TTBB, organ
9 min
American Composers Alliance
1965
Commissioned by Williams College

FIRST PERFORMANCE

Williams College, Kenneth Roberts, conductor. Williamstown, MA. April
24, 1966

W62 Remembrance (text: Hoover Rupert)

SATB, organ
4 min
Abingdon, re-issued by Peters c1968
1960

FIRST PERFORMANCE

First United Methodist Church Ann Arbor, Lester McCoy, conductor.
Ann Arbor, MI. October 2, 1960.

Memorial Day Brotherhood or general anthem

W63 A Ring of Emeralds
See: B64
SATB, pno
13 min
Peters c1981
1979
Commissioned by Cork International Choral and Folk Dance Festival.
Contains five settings of Irish verse in English

FIRST PERFORMANCE

Eastern Michigan University Madrigal Singers, Emily Lowe, conductor.
Cork International Choral and Folk Dance Festival. Cork,
Ireland. April 27, 1979

OTHER PERFORMANCES

University of Michigan Choir, Patrick Gardner, conductor. Ann Arbor,
MI. March 10, 1982

Ohio State University Choir, Maurice Casey, conductor. Columbus, OH.
October 21, 1988

Cleveland State University, Cleveland, OH. February 1984

Eastern Michigan University, Ypsilanti, MI. April 12, 1985

Cork Festival, Ireland, Eastern Michigan University, Emily Lowe,
conductor. May 8, 1985

Northern Illinois University Choir, Lawrence Burnett, director. Crane
School of Music, Potsdam College, SUNY, Potsdam, NY. Bassett
Festival.

Eastern Michigan University Madrigal Singers, Emily Lowe, conductor.
Ypsilanti, MI. June 29, 1989

W64 Sing to the Lord (text: Psalm 95)

SATB, organ
3 min
Peters c1987
1981

FIRST PERFORMANCE

Brevard College Choir, Lee B. Bratton, conductor. Brevard, NC. January
31, 1982

OTHER PERFORMANCES

University of Michigan Chamber Choir, Theo Morrison, conductor. Ann
Arbor, MI. October 21, 1988

W65 Whoe're She Be (text: Richard Crashaw)

SSA, women's chorus, pno
3 min
Peters c1989
1986

FIRST PERFORMANCE

University of Michigan Women's Glee Club, Rosalie Edwards, conductor.
Ann Arbor, MI. April 4, 1987

OTHER PERFORMANCES

Lee Bratton and his Brevard College Choir, Brevard, NC

MUSIC FOR SOLO VOICE

W66   Easter Triptych (text: Bible)

      tenor voice, 4 tpt, 4 tbn, 2 bar (euph), tuba, timp, 3 perc, cel
      15 min
      American Composers Alliance
      1958
      Commissioned by WUOM, University of Michigan, National
          Association of Educational Broadcasters

      FIRST PERFORMANCE

      Harold Haugh and ensemble, Radio Station WUOM. Ann Arbor, MI.
          February 15, 1960

W67   Four Songs (texts: William Blake, George Herbert, Edwin A. Robinson)

      high voice, pno
      10 min
      American Composers Alliance
      1953

      FIRST PERFORMANCE

      Norma Heyde, voice, Anita Bassett, piano. Ann Arbor,
          MI. November 15, 1953

W68   Jade Garden, 4 miniatures of Ancient Japanese and Chinese Poetry

soprano voice, pno
9 min
Merion, Presser c1977
1973

FIRST PERFORMANCE

Emily Lowe, Joseph Gurt, Eastern Michigan University. Ypsilante, MI.
February 8, 1976

W69   Love Songs (five) (text: anon. Greek, W. S. Landor, Anne Bradstreet,
Ralph Waldo Emerson, Henry Harrington

soprano voice, pno
13 min
Merion, Presser c1977
1975
Commissioned by Music Teachers National Association for its Centennial
Year and the American Bicentennial

FIRST PERFORMANCE

Elizabeth Mosher, soprano, Jack Roberts, piano, Music Teachers
National Association. Dallas, T . March 31, 1976

W70   Pierrot Songs (text: Albert Giraud, translated into German by
O.E.Hartleben)

soprano voice, fl, cl, vln, cello, pno
12 min
Peters c1990
1988
Commissioned by Schoenberg Institute, University of Southern
California, Los Angeles, CA

FIRST PERFORMANCE

First song premiered by Christine Schadeberg, soprano, and New York
    New Music Ensemble, Robert Black, conductor. Bing Theatre, Los
    Angeles, CA. November 7, 1988

OTHER PERFORMANCES

Second and third songs premiered by Lucy Shelton, soprano voice, and Da
    Capo Players. Los Angeles, CA. January 25, 1989

Note: Texts not used by Schoenberg in his "Pierrot Lunaire"

W71 Time and Beyond (text: Ralph Waldo Emerson, Sir Rabindranith Tagore,
     Mark Van Doren)
     See: B105
     baritone voice, cl, cello, pno
     9 min
     Peters c1980
     1973
     Commissioned by Society for Commissioning New Music

FIRST PERFORMANCE

Fritz Moses and ensemble, Eastern Michigan University. Ypsilanti, MI.
    June 20,1973

OTHER PERFORMANCES

Raymond Murcell, vocal, Da Capo Players. Carnegie Hall, New York,
    NY. March 22, 1979

W72 To Music, Three Songs (texts: Ben Jonson, Robert Herrick, William
     Billings)

     soprano or tenor voice, pno
     11 min
     Galaxy Highgate c1966
     1962
     Commissioned by Mu Phi Epsilon

FIRST PERFORMANCE

Patty Gay, soprano, John Easton, piano. American Academy. Rome, Italy. April 17, 1962

OTHER PERFORMANCES

Waldie Anderson, tenor, David Lake, piano, National Music Camp. Interlochen, MI. June 24, 1979

EDITIONS OF OLDER MUSIC

W73   Biagio Marini: Sonata for 2 Bass Trombones and Continuo

      2 b tbn, continuo
      3 min
      Brass Press
      1973

W74   Gio. Batt. Riccio: Three Canzonas

      vln or tpt, tbn, continuo
      11 min
      Musica Rara
      1979
      Edited by Glen Smith, continuo by Leslie Bassett

W75   Gio. M. Cesare: La Hieronyma

      tbn, continuo
      4 min
      King
      1972
      Edited by Glenn Smith, continuo by Leslie Bassett

W76   Daniel Speer: Sonata and Gigue

      2 vln, tbn, continuo
      7 min
      Musica Rara

1979
Edited by Glenn Smith, continuo by Leslie Bassett

ELECTRONIC MUSIC

W77 Collect (text: Leslie Bassett)

SATB, electronic tape
5 min
World Library Publications c1970
1969
Commissioned by Upsala College

FIRST PERFORMANCE

Upsala College Choir, Richard Toensing, conductor. East
        Orange, NJ. March 3, 1969

OTHER PERFORMANCES

Santa Clara Chorale, Lynn Sutleff, conductor. Santa Clara, CA. June 3,
        1979, 1983 Symposium of Contemporary Music, University Kansas.
        Lawrence, KS. March 7, 1983

W78 Three Studies in Electronic Sound

electronic
7 min
1965

FIRST PERFORMANCE

Ann Arbor, MI. October 10, 1965

W79 Triform

electronic
6 min
1966

FIRST PERFORMANCE

Ann Arbor, MI. December 3, 1966

MUSIC FOR INSTRUMENTAL
SOLO UNACCOMPANIED

W80　A Masque of Bells

　　　carillon with or without dancers
　　　13 min
　　　1980

W81　Soliloquies
　　　See: B77, D12, P21
　　　cl solo
　　　10 min
　　　Merion, Presser
　　　1976
　　　Commissioned by Robert Onofrey

　　　FIRST PERFORMANCE

　　　Robert Onofrey, clarinet. Ann Arbor, MI. February 18, 1976

　　　OTHER PERFORMANCES

　　　Michael Waddell, clarinet, University of Michigan, Ann Arbor, MI.
　　　　　January 31 and March 26, 1979
　　　1983 Symposium of Contemporary Music, University of Kansas. Larry
　　　　　Maxey, clarinet. Lawrence, KS. March 7, 1983

　　　RECORDING

　　　Mark MES 38084

W82   Suite for Unaccompanied Trombone
      See: B60, B108, B119, D14, D15
      tbn
      6 min
      Philharmonia Music c 1957, Peters c 1969
      1957

      FIRST PERFORMANCE

      Roger Davenport, trombone. Decatur, IA. May 27, 1964

      OTHER PERFORMANCES

      Peter Vivona, trombone, Northern Arizona University. Flagstaff, AZ.
            November 24, 1985
      L. Campbell, trombone, Louisiana State University. Baton Rouge, LA.
            1979
      Thomas Olcott, trombone, Juilliard School of Music. New York, NY.
            1979
      Buddy Baker, trombone, International Trombone Workshop. Nashville,
            TN

      RECORDINGS

      Crystal S 381
      Fermat FLPS 49

W83   Temperaments (five)
      See: B76
      guitar
      12 min
      Mel Bay c1984
      1979, 1983

      FIRST PERFORMANCE

      Michael Lorimer, Ann Arbor Musical Society. Ann Arbor, MI. March 26,
            1983

MUSIC FOR ORCHESTRA

Note: The number of parts that the music provides for winds or brass may be indicated by four numbers in the order that they appear on the score, such as flutes, oboes, clarinets, bassoons, (or) horns, trumpets, trombones, tuba.

W84 Celebration in Praise of Earth (assorted environmental texts)
      See: B23, B24, B25
      SATB, amplified speaker, 2 fl (piccs), ob, EH, 2 cl, 2 bssn, 3 hn, 2 tpt, 2 tbn, tuba, pno-cel, harp, 4 perc, strings
      13 min
      Peters c1971
      1970
      Commissioned by Baldwin-Wallace College for its centennial

      FIRST PERFORMANCE

      Baldwin-Wallace College Choir and Orchestra, George Poinar, conductor.
            Berea, OH. October 14, 1971

W85 Colloquy
      See: B27, B28, P21
      2 fl, picc, 2 ob, EH, 2 cl, b cl, 2 bssn, contra bssn, 4331, 4 perc, harp, cel-pno, strings
      10 min
      Peters c1969
      1968
      Commissioned by Fresno Philharmonic Orchestra

FIRST PERFORMANCE

Fresno Philharmonic, Thomas Griswold, conductor. Fresno, CA. May 23, 1969

OTHER PERFORMANCES

Kansas University Symphony, George Lawner, conductor, Symposium for Contemporary Music. Lawrence, KS. March 6, 1983

W86   Concerto for Orchestra

3333,4331, 4 perc, pno-cel, harp, strings
28 min
Peters c 1992
1991
Commissioned by Koussevitsky Foundation and Detroit Symphony Orchestra

FIRST PERFORMANCE

Detroit Symphony Orchestra, Neeme Yarvi, conductor. Detroit, February 6, 7, 8, 9, 1992

W87   Concerto for Two Pianos and Orchestra
See: B30, B31, B32, D2, P18
2 solo pno, 3232, 4231, 4 perc, strings
19 min
Peters c1977
1976
Commissioned by Midland Symphony Orchestra

FIRST PERFORMANCE

Midland Symphony Orchestra, Don Jaeger, conductor, Nelita True, piano, Fernando Laires, piano. Midland, MI. April 30, 1977

OTHER PERFORMANCES

Ann Arbor Symphony Orchestra, Edward Szabo, conductor. Ann Arbor, MI. April 29, 1979

Midland Symphony Orchestra, Don Jaeger, conductor, Kennedy Center. Washington, D.C. May 8, 1979

Cameron Grant, piano, James Winn, piano, Plymouth Symphony Orchestra, Johan Vander Merwe, conductor. Novi, MI. 16,1983

RECORDING

Advance FGR 26S

W88   Concerto Lirico for Trombone and Orchestra
See: B57, P7
solo tbn, 3232, 4231, 4 perc, harp, pno-cel, strings
18 min
Peters c1984
1983
Commissioned by Toledo Symphony Orchestra

FIRST PERFORMANCE

H. Dennis Smith, trombone, Toledo Symphony Orchestra, Zaliouk, conductor, Toledo, OH. April, 6-7, 1984

OTHER PERFORMANCES

H. Dennis Smith, trombone, Peter Britt Festival, OR. August 15, 1985
H. Dennis Smith, trombone, Bakersfield Symphony, CA. November 16, 1985

W89   Echoes from an Invisible World
See: B41, B42, B43, B58, B66, B73, B75, B104, B110, D6, P2, P3, P5, P6, P8, P9, P10, P13, P17, P19
picc, 2 fl, 2 ob, EH, 2 cl, b cl, 2 bssn, c bssn, 4431, 4 perc, harp, cel, pno, strings
18 min
Peters c1976
1974 revised 1975

Commissioned by Philadelphia Orchestra in celebration of the United States Bicentennial with funds from the National Endowment for the Arts

Winner of League of Composers ISCM National Competition

FIRST PERFORMANCE

Philadelphia Orchestra, Eugene Ormandy, conductor. Academy of Music, Philadelphia, PA. February 27, 28, March 2, October 7, 8, 9; April 28 at the May Festival, Ann Arbor, MI; May 19 at the Kennedy Center, Washington, D.C.; October 12, at CarnegieHall, New York City, 1976

OTHER PERFORMANCES

Chicago Symphony Orchestra, Charles MacKerres, conductor, October 27, 28, 29, 30, Chicago, and November 1 in Milwaukee, WI. The first movement was conducted by Gerhard Zimmerman eight times through January 10, 1977

Los Angeles Philharmonic Orchestra, Sydney Harth, conductor, Philharmonic Music Center, Los Angeles. CA. February 3,4,5,6 1977

Boston Symphony Orchestra, Kazujoshi Akiyama, conductor. Symphony Hall, Boston, MA. December 1,2,3,6 1977

Cleveland Orchestra, Lorin Maazel, conductor, Severence Hall, Cleveland, OH. January 19,21 1978

University of Michigan Symphonic Orchestra, Gustav Meier, conductor, Ann Arbor MI. February 10, 1978, and Midland Center for the Arts, Midland, MI. February 12, 1978. Also performed at Western Michigan University in Kalamazoo and Midwest Conference. Ann Arbor, MI

Baltimore Symphony, Sergiu Commissiona, conductor, Lyric Theatre, Baltimore, MD. October 17,18 1978

New York Philharmonic, Zubin Mehta, conductor, Avery Fischer Hall, New York City. February 1,2,3, 6, 1979

Baltimore Symphony Orchestra, Sergiu Commissiona, conductor. Baltimore, MD. October 24, 25, 1979

Represented the United States at the World Music Day in Tel Aviv, Israel, 1980

Western Michigan University Symphony Orchestra, Herbert Butter, conductor. Kalamazoo, MI. January 23, 1981

Netherlands Radio Orchestra, Sergiu Commissiona, conductor. Amsterdam, Netherlands. August 15, 1982

Florida State University Orchestra, John Moye, conductor. Tallahassee, FL. February 26, 1983

South Bend Symphony Orchestra, Herbert Butter, conductor. South Bend, IN. April 16, 1982

Florida Orchestra, Irwin Hoffman, conductor. Clearwater, FL. October 31; Tampa, FL, November 1; St. Petersburg, FL. November 3, 1984

Saginaw Symphony, Leo Najar, conductor. Saginaw, MI. April 27, 1985

Detroit Symphony, Gunther Herbig, conductor. Ford Auditorium and Orchestra Hall, Detroit, MI. September 26, 27, 28, 1985

Syracuse Symphony, New York, Kazuyoshi Akiyama, conductor. Syracuse, NY. January 23,24, 1987

State University College, Potsdam, NY, Crane Symphony Orchestra. February 9, 1989

RECORDING

CRI 429

W90 Five Movements for Orchestra

picc, 2 fl. 2 ob, EH, 2 cl, b cl, 2 bssn, c bssn, 4331, 3 perc, pno, strings
21 min
American Composers Alliance
1961

FIRST PERFORMANCE

RAI Symphony Orchestra of Rome, Massinio Freccia, conductor. Rome, Italy. July 5, 1962

OTHER PERFORMANCES

University of Michigan Symphony Orchestra, Josef Blatt, conductor, Contemporary Music Festival. Ann Arbor, MI. February 7, 1964

Vincent Persichetti, conductor, Michigan State University Orchestra, East
Lansing, MI, Tri-state Composers Symposium. April 20, 1964

W91 Forces

solo vln, solo cello, solo pno, 2 fl-picc, ob, EH, cl
Eb cl, EH contra cl, 2 bssn, 3221, 4 perc, strings
12 min
Peters c1973
1972
Commissioned by Drake University

FIRST PERFORMANCE

Drake University Orchestra, Thomas Griswold, conductor.
Des Moines, IA. May 1, 1973

W92 From a Source Evolving
See: B50, P16, P24
3 fl, (3rd on picc), 2 ob, EH, 2 cl. b cl, 2 bssn
4 hn,3 tpt, 3 tbn, tba, 4 perc, harp, pno, strings
14 min
Peters c1986
1985
Commissioned by three Michigan orchestras: Traverse, Midland and
Saginaw, with funds from the National Endowment for the Arts in
memory of Bassett's father

FIRST PERFORMANCE

Midland Symphony Orchestra, Neal Gittleman,conductor.
Midland, MI. November 1, 1986

OTHER PERFORMANCES

Saginaw Symphony Orchestra, Leo Najer, conductor,
Saginaw, MI. November 22, 1986
University Philharmonia, Leo Najer, conductor. Ann
Arbor, MI. November 24, 1986

Grand Rapids Symphony, Catherine Comet, conductor.
Grand Rapids, MI. November 18 and 19, 1988
Several subsequent performances to date

W93 Variations for Orchestra
See: B117, B122, D18, P2
picc, fl, ob, EH, cl, bssn, c bssn, 4231, 3 or more perc, cel-pno, harp,
strings
23 min
Peters c1966
1963
Pulitzer Prize in Music, 1966

FIRST PERFORMANCE

RAI Orchestra of Rome, Italy, Ferrucio Scaglia, conductor. Rome, Italy.
July 6, 1963

U. S. PREMIERE

Philadelphia Orchestra, Eugene Ormandy, conductor. Philadelphia, PA.
October 22-23, 1965

OTHER PERFORMANCES

UNESCO, International Rostrum of Composers, Paris, France, 1966
Major orchestra performances in 1966 and 1967 include:
Philadelphia Orchestra, Eugene Ormandy, conductor.
Interlochen Arts Academy, Thor Johnson, conductor.
Detroit Symphony Orchestra, Sixten Ehrling, conductor. Rockefeller
Grant for Orchestra Symposium.
Indianapolis Symphony Orchestra, Isler Soloman, conductor.
New England Conservatory Orchestra, Richard Pittman, conductor.
Boston, MA
There were many more major performances through the years

RECORDING

CRI SD 203

ORGAN MUSIC

W94 Four Statements

  organ
  10 min
  American Composers Alliance c1964
  1964

  FIRST PERFORMANCE

  Marilyn Mason, organ. Ann Arbor, MI. February 13, 1965

W95 Liturgies (six movements)
  See: B71, B87, B102
  organ
  20 min
  Peters c1984
  1980
  Commissioned by Marilyn Mason

  FIRST PERFORMANCE

  Marilyn Mason, organ, 20th Ann Arbor Organ Conference. Ann Arbor,
    MI. October 20, 1980

  OTHER PERFORMANCES

  John Peterson, organ, Memphis State University. Memphis, TN.
    February 25, 1982

James Nissen, organ, Zion Lutheran Church (recital). Ann Arbor, MI.
    April 4, 1982
Carl Angelo, organ, Kent State University. Kent, OH. March 2, 1984
Paul Kosower, organ, University of Wisconsin. Eau Claire, WI. March 3,
    1989

W96   Toccata

organ
4 min
American Composers Alliance c1957
1953

FIRST PERFORMANCE

Marilyn Mason, organ. New York, NY. July 21, 1955

W97   Voluntaries (three)

organ
8 min
American Composers Alliance c1967
1958

FIRST PERFORMANCE

Mary Stubbins, organ. Ann Arbor, MI. November 2, 1958

PIANO MUSIC

W98 Concerto for Two Pianos and Orchestra
     See: B30, B31, B32, D2, P18
     2 solo pno, 3232, 4231, 4 perc, strings
     19 min
     Peters
     1976
     Commissioned by Midland Symphony Orchestra

FIRST PERFORMANCE

Midland Symphony, Don Jaeger, conductor, Nelita True, piano,
     Fernando Laires, piano. Midland, MI. April 30, 1977

OTHER PERFORMANCES

Ann Arbor Symphony Orchestra, Edward Szabo, conductor, Ann Arbor,
MI. April 29, 1979.
Midland Symphony Orchestra, Don Jaeger, conductor, Kennedy Center.
     Washington, D.C. May 8, 1979
Cameron Grant, piano, James Winn, piano, Plymouth Symphony
     Orchestra, Novi, MI. Johan Vander Merwe, conductor. October 16,
     1983

RECORDING

Advance FGR 26S

W99   Configurations (five)

pno
12 min
Peters c1988
1987
Commissioned by Music Teachers Association of California

FIRST PERFORMANCE

Music Teachers Association of California, San Jose, California. July 5,
    1987. Premiered by five young pianists

W100 Elaborations

pno
8 min
Peters c1973
1966

FIRST PERFORMANCE

Wesley True, piano. Warrensburg, MO. November 2, 1970

W101 Mobile
See: B56
pno
2 min
Hinshaw
1961

FIRST PERFORMANCE

John Eaton, piano. Rome, Italy. December 23, 1962

W102 Preludes (seven)
pno
18 min
Peters c1988
1984

Commissioned by colleagues of Benning Dexter

FIRST PERFORMANCE

Benning Dexter, piano, University of Michigan. Ann Arbor, MI. February 16, 1985

OTHER PERFORMANCES

Steve McColley, piano, University of Southern Florida. Tampa, FL. February 25, 1985. Bassett Concert

Michael Coonrod, Interlochen Arts Academy. Interlochen, MI. March 16, 1985

Nancy Saxon, piano, Festival Louisiana State University. Baton Rouge, LA. February 28, 1986

Benning Dexter, piano, several performances in 1987 including Music Teachers National Association, New York City, March 22, 1987. In 1988 he performed *Preludes* at Sierra Heights College, MI; Central Michigan University, Mt. Pleasant, MI; Society for Musical Arts, Womens City Club, Ann Arbor, MI; Kerrytown Concert House, Ann Arbor, MI

Barbara Wimunc-Pearson, University of Wisconsin. Eau Claire, WI. March 2, 1989. For Bassett Programs.

Benning Dexter, Eastern Michigan University. Ypsilanti, MI. October 12, 1989

W103 Six Piano Pieces

pno
12 min
American Composers Alliance
1951
Commissioned by Music Teachers Association of California

FIRST PERFORMANCE

Lillian Megidow, piano. Los Angeles, CA. April 27, 1952

Discography

Instrumental and orchestral compositions by Bassett appear on many published recordings which contain twentieth century composers. There are no choral or vocal works by Bassett on published recordings. Excellent comments written by Bassett are often found on record jackets. In addition, analytical comments by reviewers of Bassett's music, and occasional comments about the performers may be found there.

Recordings include two instrumental solo works, one for clarinet, *Soliloquies,* (D12), and one for trombone, *Suite for Unaccompanied Trombone,* (D14 and D15). There are three selections for full orchestra, *Concerto for Two Pianos and Orchestra,* (D2), *Echoes from an Invisible World,* (D6), and *Variations for Orchestra,* (D18).

Chamber music recordings of Bassett's music include: *Clarinet Duets,* (D1), *Dialogues for Oboe and Piano,* (D4), *Duo Concertante,* (D5), *Music for Cello and Piano,* (D7), *Music for Saxophone and Piano,* (D8 and D9), *Quintet for Piano and Strings,* (D10), *Sextet for Piano and Strings,* (D11), *Sounds Remembered,* (D13), *Trio for Viola, Clarinet and Piano,* (D16), and *Trio for Violin, Clarinet and Piano,* (D17).

A discography arranged in alphabetical order by title appears on subsequent pages.

D1   Clarinet Duets
     Mark Educational Records
     Paul Drushler, clarinet, Larry Combs, clarinet
     Mark MES 57590

D2   Concerto for Two Pianos and Orchestra
     Advance Recordings (American Society of University Composers
     Recording Series)
     Fernando Laires, piano, Nelita True, piano, Midland Symphony
     Orchestra, Don Th. Jaeger, conductor
     Advance FGR 26S

D3   Designs, Images and Textures
     Golden   Crest   (Educational   Record   Reference   Library,   c/o
          Franco Colombo)
     University of Michigan Band, William Revelli, conductor
     CRS 4214

D4   Dialogues for Oboe and Piano
     Crystal
     Harry Sargous, oboe, Robert Conway, piano.
     Crystal CD 326

D5   Duo Concertante
     ACA Digital Recordings, Atlanta
     Kenneth Fischer, alto saxophone, Richard Zimber, piano
     CM 20003-3

D6   Echoes from an Invisible World
     Composers Recordings, Inc.
     Baltimore   Symphony   Orchestra,   Sergiu   Commissiona,
          conductor
     CRI 429

D7   Music for Cello and Piano
     Composers Recordings, Inc.
     Jerome Jelinek, cello, Joseph Gurt, piano
     CRI SD 311

D8   Music for Saxophone and Piano
     New World Records

Donald Sinta, saxophone, Ellen Weckler, piano. "New Music for Virtuosos"
New World NW 209

D9   Music for Saxophone and Piano
Open Loop Records
Phil Delibert, saxophone, and Mary Senellie, piano
Open Loop no. 1

D10 Withdrawn

D11 Sextet for Piano and Strings
Composers Recordings, Inc. (Naumburg Recording Prize)
Concord String Quartet, John Graham, viola, Gil Kalish, piano
CRI 323

D12 Soliloquies
Mark Educational Records
Elsa Ludewig-Verdehr, clarinet solo
Mark MES 38084

D13 Sounds Remembered
Desto Records, Inc.
Charles Treger, violin, Samuel Sanders, piano
Desto DC 7142

D14 Suite for Unaccompanied Trombone
Crystal (Crystal Records Recital Series)
Ralph Sauer, trombone
Crystal S 381

D15 Suite for Unaccompanied Trombone
Fermat
Christian Lindberg, trombone
Fermat FLPS 49

D16 Trio for Viola, Clarinet and Piano
Composers Recording, Inc.
Walter Trampler, viola, Charles Russo, clarinet, Douglas Nordi, piano
CRI 148

D17   Trio for Violin, Clarinet and Piano
      Leonarda Records
      Verdehr Trio
      Leonarda LE 326 compact disk

D18   Variations for Orchestra
      Composers Recordings, Inc. (Pulitzer Prize)
      Orchestra of Radio Zurich, Jonathan Sternberg, conductor
      CRI SD 203

Annotated Reviews of Performances and Concerts

P1   "Arts and Films, The Lively American Concert Touch." [Review], by
Michael Steinberg, *Boston Evening Globe,* Tuesday, July 20, 1976, p.27.

"The inclusion of an American work at each Monday evening Harvard
Summer School concert is producing lively results... Last week we heard
the beautiful *Lament for Oedipus* by Seymour Shifrin, who teaches at
Brandeis... It was fascinating to hear yesterday, in Leslie Bassett's *Sextet
for Piano and Strings,* the working out on a larger scale of a similar idea,
in an abstract context of course, and in an altogether different musical
language... The *Sextet* completed in 1972, is in four movements; The first
two begin energeticallybut subside into a kind of a tense condition of rest,
the third is very slow, the last is sheer fury. The music sounds rich and at
the same time defined like very tough sculpture. Bassett uses special effects
-- the slow movement winds down to the cellist's drumming on his
instrument with with his fingers, and the pianist sometimes reaches into
the case to pluck or stop the strings -- but this happens with discretion and
always as an extension rather than a disruption of normal sound."

P2   "Baltimore Symphony Produces Fine LPs." CRI Records SD 429,
[Review] by James E. Harvey, Journal Arts Writer, *Flint Journal,*
February 16, 1981.

In his review of the sound recording in the *Flint Journal*, February 16, 1981, James E. Harvey likens *Echoes from an Invisible World* to Bassett's prize-winning *Variations for Orchestra* in its flair for color and energetic feeling for putting characteristic phrases and rhythms under a variety of lights. The three-movement work is an abstract expansion of the words of Giuseppe Mazzini, leader of the 19th-century Italian Risorgimento, that music is "the echo from an invisible world." He praises Bassett's command of orchestral sound and his masterful sense of proportion.

P3   "Cellist Subs With Great Success." [Review] by John Guinn, *Detroit Free Press,* Saturday, September 28, 1985.

Following a surprise substitution by Nathaniel Rosen playing William Schumann's cello concerto, when Yo-Yo Ma's wife had a baby girl, the Detroit Symphony Orchestra played Bassett's *Echoes from an Invisible World* with Bassett in the audience receiving tribute.

P4   "Chestnut Brass Company Delivers a Lively, Witty Show."[Review] by Gerald Brennan, *Ann Arbor News,* Monday, May 15, 1989.

The Chestnut Brass quintet presented authentic performances of 500 years of music on the evening being reviewed. "Bassett's *Brass Quintet,* a piece he wrote for the Chestnut Brass Company saved the night from becoming little more than an interesting and witty trip to the museum. It is a beautifully balanced five- movement piece...nicely dispatched by the CBC, and only the garbling of some important information in the last movement proved bothersome [and it] should float to the top ranks with each exposure."

P5   "Composer Entices Audience Into..." [Review] by John Phipps, *Saginaw News,* April 27, 1985.

"It advanced inexorably into a musical life of its own and he called it by the name that had so impressed him: *Echoes from an Invisible World.* The phrase was part of an unusual definition of music by Italian freedom fighter and writer Guiseppe Mazzini. *Echoes* will open the concert. It's accessible music. Leo Nader said it's very articulate music and it's very well crafted. Everything unfolds in a rational and logical pattern. I was trying to simply capture the magic and beauty of music, Bassett said."

P6   "Concerto for Trombone Is Premiered in Toledo." [Review] by Boris Nelson, *The Blade,* Toledo, Ohio. Sunday, April 8, 1984.

Concerto Lirico, 18 minutes, for trombone and orchestra was commissioned by the Toledo Symphony and premiered with Yuval Zaliouk, conductor, on April 6, 1984, at Masonic Auditorium in Toledo, Ohio. The new trombone concerto was written for its principal trombonist, H. Dennis Smith, by Mr. Smith's University of Michigan colleague and well-known composer, Leslie Bassett. In this lengthy review of the concert by Boris Nelson, he credits the composer with a "well crafted piece by a composer who knows his orchestration and wrote most indigenously for the solo instrument, music which was beautifully played...a lyrical voice, set against an often busy orchestral one."

P7   "Echoes from an Invisible World." CRI Records, SD 429, produced by Carter Harman, [Review] by Roger Dettmor, *Fanfare,* March April, 1981, p.68-69.

"Now at last we have Bassett's fastidiously made *poema*, in three sections without pause, inspired by a description of music by the Italian author and patriot,Giuseppe Mazzini. But we don't have it in a performance which is severely disappointing, by Eugene Ormandy and the Philadelphia Orchestra who commissioned *Echoes.* CRI cover notes report that Sergiu Commissiona programmed the work in Baltimore during the 1977-79 season. But the playing on disc belies any such degree of familiarity with, or mastery of, the music's difficulties. I don't mean to imply that Bassett's lucid and euphonious music is anywhere as dense as Carter's Symphony, or as wildly chancy as *Renga With Apartment House 1776,* which John Cage stuck to Ozawa and the Boston Symphony."

P8   "Echoes from an Invisible World." [Review], by Jocelyn Mackey, *Sigma Alpha Iota Quarterly: Pan Pipes,* Winter 1982, p.15.

"Dr. Bassett comments that much of this music is derived from ideas implanted within the score which at first seem insignificant, such as the opening three-chord piano figure whose twelve tones recur in many guises throughout the work. The principle of unfolding and growth from small elements is basic to the work, as is the principle of return to them. This piece should appeal immediately to a large number of listeners; it is a composition which will yield new delights each time it is heard," wrote Mackey in her review of Composers Recordings, Inc. CRI 429.

P9   "Echoes, Beethoven Rock Rafters." [Review] by John Phipps, *Saginaw News,* April 28?, 1985.

"The Saginaw Symphony Orchestra and friends presented a sensory delight in Heritage Theater Saturday to end the orchestra's 50th season... The orchestra titillated a nearly full house with Leslie Bassett's *Echoes from an Invisible World* before reaching back to rock the rafters with Beethoven."

P10   "Echoes, by Mehta." [Review] by Shirley Fleming, *New York Post,* February 2, 1979.

The New York Philharmonic Orchestra, Zubin Mehta, conducting, opened its concert on February 1, 1979 with Bassett's *Echoes from an Invisible World.* Fleming describes it as "notably delicate in its handling of orchestral timbres and colors, producing shimmering surfaces and transparent webs out of very small fragments of melody."

P11   "Eloquent New Music--and for Free." [Review] by Richard Dyer, *The Boston Globe,* Tuesday, November 2, 1976.

"Harvard University's annual series of free new-music concerts was presented under the sponsorship of the Fromm Music Foundation, music by Leslie Bassett, Andrew Imbre and Jacob Druckman at Sanders Theatre last night. The Pro Arte Group was the nucleus for the Bassett piece as well. Violinists Norman Paulu and Martha Francis, violinist Richard Blum and cellist Harry Karp were supplemented by Scott Nickrenz, viola, and Richard Kogan, piano, who had played in the summer performance. The sextet is wonderful imaginative craft at work on interesting materials in it."

P12   "Flute, Piano Work Illuminating." [Review] by Jeffrey Magee, *Ann Arbor News,* Monday, February 12, 1990.

Review of *Illuminations for Flute and Piano* was performed by the Bryan and Keys Duo at the Faculty Artists Concert at Rackham Auditorium. The piece was dedicated to the Duo: Keith Bryan, flute, and Karen Keys, piano.

P13   "Music From Romantic, Contemporary Eras Provides Fine Masterworks Fare." [Review] by Mary Nic Shenk, *St. Petersburg Times,* October 31, 1984.

Florida Orchestra, Irwin Hoffman, conductor, Clearwater, Florida, playing *Echoes From an Invisible World.* "Throughout there is a haunting, come hither aural effect to the music and the enveloping warmth as the musical tones and lines rise and fall. Many of the darting, stabbing sounds appear to be random as they seemingly emerge from nowhere. The close intervals, seconds, which would normally be timed dissonances, don't sound harsh. There are distinct and diverse colors with beautiful sustained sounds, a glorious English horn solo, magnificent brass choir and lovely string melodies, all stressing a wide dynamic range and frequent, striking tempo changes."

P14   "Music Needs Merchandizing." [Review] by Richard Devinney, *Grand Rapids Press,* Monday, May 17, 1982.

"The Grand Rapids Musica Nova Ensemble, Barrett Kalellis, conductor, with baritone Theodore Rulfs, at the Race Street Gallery, performed *Eight Songs for a Mad King* by Davies, *Five Pieces* by Cowell, *Sextet for Flutes, Clarinets and Strings* by Bassett, and *Tic* by Albright, Saturday evening. The question [does music need merchandizing] seemed philosophical enough to elicit a fuzzy, harmless answer, but composer Leslie Bassett replied quickly and directly. I blame the orchestras...the vast majority of classical music fans aren't even aware of what is being done by the most creative 20th century composers!"

P15   "Music Noted in Brief." [Review] by Tim Page, *New York Times,* Tuesday, February 22, 1983.

Bassett's *Concerto Grosso,* was played by the Michigan Wind Ensemble composed of students and faculty from the the University of Michigan, under the direction of H. Robert Reynolds, at the Alice Tully Hall, New York City, in February 1983.

P16   "Music Wonderful Despite Sloppiness." [Review] by Eric Nisula, *Midland Daily News,* Monday, November 3, 1986.

An excellent review of the Midland Symphony Orchestra's premiere performance, with guest conductor, Neal Gittleman, of Leslie Bassett's

From a Source Evolving, on November 1, 1986, written by critic Eric Nisula. Nisula comments on the performance and the nuances of the music. The composer, who was present, applauded the orchestra and was in turn applauded by the symphony members and the audience.

P17   "Orchestra Plays Salute to Bicen." [Review] by Daniel Webster, *Philadelphia Inquirer,* Saturday, February 28, 1976, p.4A.

Daniel Webster reviewed the Philadelphia Orchestra premier of *Echoes from an Invisible World* in the *Philadelphia Inquirer,* describing the project, the music and the performance.

P18   "Premiere Highlights Year-end Concert at Midland."[Review] by James W. Henderson, *The Saginaw News,* Monday, May 2, 1977.

The review of the Midland Symphony Orchestra premiere of *Concerto for Two Pianos and Orchestra* describes the reviewer's reaction to the music and describes the composition of the piece.

P19   "A Prophet With Honor." [Review] by Nancy Malitz, *Detroit News,* September 26, 1985.

The Detroit Symphony Orchestra performed Bassett's *Echoes from an Invisible World,* September 26, 27, 28, 1985, in Detroit.

In an interview before the concert, Bassett told the story of receiving a tape from the superb RAI rendition of *Variations for Orchestra,* an extremely successful premiere, in Rome. When he returned to Ann Arbor he played the tape for James Wallace, dean of the University of Michigan School at that time. "Jim called up Ormandy on the spot and said, Gene, you've got to play this piece. And that's really how it happened. Ormandy just slid it into the repertory for 1965."

P20   "Pulitzer Prize-Winning Composer Lives with the Sounds of Music." [Review] by Ann Marie Martin, *Huntsville Times,* June 3, 1990.

Leslie Bassett, Pulitzer Prize winner, appeared in Huntsville, Alabama, in 1990 for the premiere of his *Almighty Eternal,* a piece commissioned by the University of Alabama, Huntsville. In addition to *Almighty Eternal* the University's Concert Choir performed his *Collect,* a prayer against war.

P21   "Riding the Winds of Contemporary Music." [Review] by Michael Huebner, *Kansas City Times,* March 13, 1983.

At the annual Symposium of Contemporary Music, University of Kansas, Lawrence, the year's guests were Pulitzer Prize-winning composer Leslie Bassett, flutist Harvey Sollberger, and music historian and critic Lance Brunner. Huebner wrote, "Mr. Bassett has written for a wide range of media, from solo instruments to electronic tape to full orchestra. Among the works by Mr. Bassett performed at the symposium were *Soliloquies* (1978) for solo clarinet, a short almost schizophrenic work that changed in mood from aggressive to flowing to abrasive to lyrical; the *Colloquy* for orchestra (1968); and the *Nonet* for piano and winds."

P22   "A Saxophonist With an Affinity for Michigan." [Review] by Allan Kozinn, *New York Times,* Monday, May 21, 1990.

Expert saxophonist Gary Louie performed *Music for Saxophone and Piano,* written by Bassett in 1968, in a moving concert of contemporary music at Gould Hall, New York City, on May 17, 1990. All of the works performed were written by composers associated with the University of Michigan School of Music where Louie studied. This is a high commendation to Bassett, who is head of the Composition Department at the University. Louie's warm tones and carefully shaped phrases were highlighted by a beautiful vibrato and comprehension of the saxophone's color and range.

P23   "Style Varied, But Quality All Was High." [Review] by Julie Ridenour, *Grand Rapids Press,* Saturday, November 19, 1988.

Review of the Grand Rapids Symphony Orchestra which featured Bassett's work first on the program.

P24   "World Premiere Work, Arden Trio Highlights Saturday's MSO Concert." [Review] by Diane Niedzweicki, *Midland Daily News,* Wednesday, October 29, 1986.

The world premiere of Bassett's *From a Source Evolving* was performed November 1, 1986, by the Midland Symphony Orchestra, Neal Gittleman, guest conductor. It was commissioned by a grant from the National Endowment for the Arts for the Midland, Saginaw, and Traverse

Orchestras. In a telephone interview from Ann Arbor, Bassett said the single-movement *From a Source Evolving* is influenced by one four-note chord from beginning to end. The chord moves in and out of the piece, Bassett said, and appears in various guises throughout the work lending logic and consistency.

Bibliography

B1   "AmerAllegro." *Pan Pipes, Sigma Alpha Iota Quarterly*, Annual Winter
      Issues, v.46, no.2-v.72, no.2, 1954-1979.

      "AmerAllegro" preceded "American Composer Update" in the winter
      issues of *Pan Pipes*. M. K. Kyle was the editor. Over 200 contemporary
      composers are featured here.

B2   "American Academy Institute Ceremonial." *BMI Many Worlds of Music*,
      v. 22, no.2, 1981.

      News item.

B3   "American Composer Update." *Pan Pipes,* Sigma Alpha Iota Quarterly,
      Annual Winter Issues, 1954 (AmerAllegro)-1991 and continue.

      Beginning in 1954 Leslie Bassett's activities have appeared annually in the
      winter issue. Each issue presents Bassett's activity for the year just
      completed under the following headings:

      Premieres: title of the composition, date and location, sponsor,
      performers, performing groups, conductors, commissions, and related
      information; Performances: (other than the premiere); Publications:
      publisher; Recordings: record publisher; News: lectures, awards and other
      activity.

This annual SAI feature includes over 200 contemporary composers and is sponsored by Sigma Alpha Iota Philanthropies, Inc. The title page of the *Pan Pipes* states, "Sigma Alpha Iota, international music fraternity for women, was organized in 1903 to form chapters of music students and musicians who shall by their influence and their musical interest uphold the highest ideals of a musical education; to raise the standard of productive musical work among the women students of colleges, conservatories and universities."

B4   "American Music Committee." *American Music Teacher*, v. 16, no.2, p.25, 1966.

Biography and portrait.

B5   *American Music Recordings, A Discography of 20th Century U. S. Composers.* Edited by Carol J. Oja. New York: Institute for Studies in American Music, Conservatory of Music, Brooklyn College of the City of New York, 1982.

Works of Bassett are listed.

B6   *American Record Guide.* Millbrook, New York: Salem Research. Issued bimonthly.

This periodical lists recordings which are available for purchase.

B7   Archibald, Bruce. "Bassett's Manual of Sixteenth Century Counterpoint." *Music Library Association Notes,* v.25, no.1, p.43-4, September 1968.

Archibald reviews the book describing the purpose, organization, and contents of the *Manual.*

"This small manual is a valuable pedological document ... placing the larger portion of his investment in music rather than words ... a healthy investment."

He notes a "lack of an explanation of 16th century notation and modern transcription, canons, cantus firmus technique, and the fact that the use of motives is briefly mentioned, but in line with the announced purpose of the manual he agrees that it leaves the teacher free to mold his own course of instruction."

B8   Ayscue, Brian. "Music for Saxophone and Piano." *The Saxophone Symposium,* North American Saxophone Alliance, VIII, no.1, p.20, 1983.

Detailed description of the four movements in *Music,*"a work written in a free chromatic style, employing dissonances and color, but not without references to tonal centers. The extended range for the saxophonist, and some special effects for pianist, contribute to the music, which is alternately spatially free or intently driving."

B9   *Baker's Biographical Dictionary of Musicians.* 7th ed. Revised by Nicolas Slonimsky. New York: Schirmer Books, 1984. p. 169.

"In his music he pursues the ideal of structural logic within the judicial limits of the modern school of composition, with some serial elements discernible in his use of thematic rhythms and motivic periodicity," comments Slonimsky in this biography of Bassett.

B10   *Band Music Guide, Alphabetical Listing of Composers and Titles of All Band Music.* 8th ed. Evanston, Il.: Instrumental Company, 1982.

Lists music available for performance by bands.

B11   Bassett, Leslie. "Form in Tonal Music." *Journal of Music Theory,* v. 9, no.2, p.318-9, 1965.

Review by Bassett of Douglas Green's *Form in Tonal Music,* New York: Holt, Rinehart and Winston, 1965. 320 p.

Bassett says," In summary, *Form in Tonal Music* is carefully assembled, detailed and systematic text in the Goetchius tradition, beautifully prepared and printed, filled with examples, well-planned for school and reference use, and somewhat more concerned with showing the formal design of music than with revealing the delights of the inner structure."

B12   Bassett, Leslie. *Manual of Sixteenth-Century Counterpoint.* New York: Appleton-Century-Crofts, 1967. 55p.

This manual contains facsimiles of 16th century scores, an abundance of examples, principles of melody of two part writing, invertible counterpoint in two parts, counterpoint in three parts, multi-voiced writing, and table of supplementary examples. Available in music libraries.

B13   "Bassett To Be Honored at Ninth ITW." by Ben Ivey. *International Trombone Association Newsletter,* v.6, no.3, p.2, April 1979.

Announcement of coming honor at the annual International Trombone Workshop.

B14   Beaumont, F. *Viola-Diskographie/Discographie sur l'Alto.* Kassel, Germany: Bärenreiter-Verlag, 1973.

Bassett is listed in this German work.

B15   Boroff, Edith. "Leslie Bassett." *Asterisk,* ii\22, p.8, 1976. Published in Omaha, NE. Available on microfilm.

Contains a biography and list of works.

B16   *Boston Composers Project: A Bibliography of Contemporary Music.* Edited by Linda I. Solow. Cambridge: MIT Press, 1983.

This bibliography was a project of sixteen Boston-area music libraries (BAML) to coordinate the collection and documentation of music by Boston composers, 1975-1980. It includes Bassett.

B17   Boston Public Library. *Dictionary Catalog of the Music Collection, Boston Public Library.* Boston: G. K. Hall., 1972. 20 volumes.

Catalog gives holdings for Bassett's works owned by the Boston library.

B18   British Library. *The Catalog of Printed Music in the British Library To 1980.* New York: K.S. Sauer, 1987. v.4, p.57.

Catalog gives holdings for Bassett's works owned by the British Library.

B19   Brooks, Richard. "Concerto da Camera." *Music Library Association Notes,* v.45, no.1, p.154, September 1988.

Brooks reviews *Concerto da Camera,* Bassett's work for trumpet and chamber ensemble, in conjunction with other instrumental-solo-with-ensemble music by Carr, Collarafi, Madsen, Osborne, Arnold, Muldowney, Orr, and Sallinen. There is an explosion of new works for virtuoso performaes and their vastly improved instruments.

B20   Butterworth, Neil. *A Dictionary of American Composers.* New York: Garland Publishing, Inc., 1984. pp.27-28.

Biography of Bassett and list of his works.

B21   Campora, Randy. "Leslie Bassett Retires." *ITA Journal, International Trombone Association,* v. 19, no.4, p.13, 1992.

Reviews the occasion.

B22   Camus, Raoul. "Colors and Contours." *Music Library Association Notes,* v.43, no.2, p.413-4, December 1986.

Camus discusses the continuing concern of the CBDNA (College Band Director National Association) in commissioning band compositions to enable a high level of proficiency in performance for smaller college and community groups. He describes other symphonic band works in addition to Bassett's recently commissioned *Colors and Contours.*

B23   "Celebration in Praise of Earth, Premieres." *Music Education Journal,* v.58, p.94, January 1972.

This journal regularly published lists of premiere performances of new music.

B24   "Celebration in Praise of Earth." *Music Journal,* v.29, no.10, p.77, December 1971.

Celebration in Praise of Earth takes its text from many classical sources. Baldwin-Wallace College commissioned the work to celebrate its 125th anniversary year.   The premiere was at the College, Berea, Ohio, performed by the College's Symphony Orchestra, George Poiner, conductor, on October 14, 1971.

B25   *Choral Music In Print, Master Index, 1991.* (Music in Print Series, v.CHX) Philadelphia: Musicdata, Inc., 1991

One of a series of music-in-print bibliographies useful for locating purchasing information, includes Bassett.

B26   Cochran, Alfred W. "Duo Concertante." *Music Library Association Notes,* v.46, no.1, p.223-4, September 1990.

A detailed, critical review of this composition.

B27   "Colloquy, Premiere." *BMI, Many Worlds of Music,* p.43, Summer 1969.

Announcement of the premiere performance of this work.

B28   "Colloquy, First Performance." *World Music,* v. 11, no.4, p.78, 1969.

Review of *Colloquy* performance.

B29 "Concerto for Two Pianos and Orchestra." *Clavier*, v.16, no.7, p.39, 1977.

News article on the premiere on April 30, 1977, with a picture of Nelita True and Fernando Laires, pianists, on either end and Leslie Bassett and Don Th. Jaeger, conductor, between them. The work was commissioned by the Midland Symphony Orchestra, Michigan, in honor of Alden B. Dow.

B30 "Concerto for Two Pianos and Orchestra, Concerning ALS Members." *Journal of American Liszt Society*, v.16, no.7, 1977.

News announcement.

B31 "Concerto for Two Pianos and Orchestra." *Symphony News*, v.28, no.3, p.47+, 1977.

News announcement.

B32 *Contemporary American Authors, A Biographical Dictionary*. 2d ed. Compiled by E. Ruth Anderson. Boston: G.K. Hall, 1982. p.31.

Includes a biography and list of Bassett's works.

B33 *Contemporary Composers*. Edited by Brian Morton and Pamela Collins. Chicago and London: St. James Press, 1992.

Excellent biography and complete list of works.

B34 *Contemporary Music Project. CMP Library Catalog*. 3v. Washington, D.C.: CMP, 1970.

Published music for schools, community, and amateur orchestras, choirs, bands, and ensembles. This catalog contained ten years of creative efforts, listed description, two pages from the score, and purchasing information. Music Educators National Conference, Ford Foundation Grant.

B35   Creighton, James Lesley. G. *Discopaedia of the Violin (1889-1971)*. Toronto: University of Toronto Press, 1991.

Lists Bassett's violin music.

B36   Daniels, David. *Orchestral Music, A Handbook*. Metuchen, N.J.: Scarecrow Press, Inc., 1991.

A handbook for instrumental musicians.

B37   Devinney, Richard. "Music Needs Merchandising." *Grand Rapids Press*, Monday, May 17, 1982.

During an interview at a pre-concert, meet-the-composer session prior to a Grand Rapids Symphony performance, Bassett was asked why the vast majority of classical music fans aren't even aware of what is being done by the most creative 20th-century composers. His response was succinct, "I blame the orchestras." A lively discussion which also includes composer William Albright follows.

B38   *Dictionary of Contemporary Music*. John Vinton, editor. New York: E. P. Dutton and Co., c1974.

Basset's biography, principal compositions, bibliography.

B39   *Dictionary of New Music, Composium, An Annual Index of Contemporary Compositions*. Sedro Wooley, WA: Crystal Musicwork.

Bassett appears in 1972, 1978-1981, 1983, and continuing issues.
The dictionary lists short biography, list of compositions, title, date, published, number of movements, instrumentation, duration, grade of difficulty, publisher.

B40   Eagon, Angelo. *Concert Music by American Composers.* 2d ed. Metuchen, NJ: Scarecrow Press, Inc., 1969. 2nd Supplement to 2d ed.

Contains entries of Bassett's music.

B41   "Echoes From an Invisible World. Premieres." *Music Education Journal,* v.62, no.2. p.14, April 1976.

News of premieres.

B42   "Echoes From an Invisible World, Premiere." *Symphony News,* v.27, no.2, p.38, 1976.

News of premiere.

B43   "Echoes From an Invisible World, 76 Bicentennial Report." *BMI, Many Worlds of Music,* p.32-5, Spring 1976.

Reports premieres and commissions.

B44   Everett, Tom. "10 Questions, 270 Answers." *Composer Magazine,* v.10-11, no.5, p.57-103, 1980.

Ten pertinent questions were sent to each of twenty seven composers, including Bassett, by Tom Everett of Harvard University, Cambridge, MA. None had access to the others answers. Questions and the answers of each composer are printed here. It is interesting to peruse the replies of these well-known contemporary composers.

B45   Everett, Tom, and others. "Five questions, 40 Answers." *Composer, (U.S.),* v.3, no.2, p.50-59, 1972.

Discussion of questions and their answers by composers.

B46   Ewen, David. *American Composers*, a biographical dictionary. New York: G. P. Putnam's Sons, 1982. p.39-41.

A lengthy biography, list of works.

B47   Finney, R. L. "Leslie Bassett." *BMI, Many Worlds of Music*, p. 16, July, 1966.

Contains biography and portrait.

B48   "Five Love Songs, Reports from Member Organizations." *National Music Council*, v.35, no.2, p.26, 1976.

News article includes Bassett work.

B49   "Five Questions, Thirty Five Answers." *Composer (U.S.)*, v.9, p. 18-27, 1977-1978.

Answers to five questions related to contemporary music are given by Bassett and six other contemporary composers.

B50   "From a Source Evolving, 1986-87 Premieres and Season Highlights." *Symphony Magazine*, v.37, no.5, p.20, 1986.

Includes Bassett's work, *From a Source Evolving.*

B51   Gifford, Virginia Snodgrass. *Music for Oboe, Oboe D Amore, and English Horn, A Bibliography.* Westport, CT: Greenwood Press, Music Reference Collection, Number 1, 1983.

A bibliography of materials at the Library of Congress, Washington, D.C.

B52   Gilbert, Richard. *The Clarinetists' Solo Repertoire: A Discography.* New York: Grenadilla Society, 1972.

Recommendations for performers selection.

B53   Greene, Frank. *Composers on Record.* Metuchen, NJ: Scarecrow Press, Inc., 1985.

Excellent index to use in locating bibliographical information in reference books on 14,000 composers whose music has been recorded. books.

B54   Guinn, J. "Concerto for Orchestra, premiere." *American Record Guide,* v. 55, no.4, p.62, 1992.

Review of the premiere of *Concerto for Orchestra* with the Detroit Sympnony Orchestra and conducted by Neeme Järvi.

B55   *Harvard Concise Dictionary of Music.* Compiled by Don Michal Randall. Cambridge and London: Belknap Press of Harvard University Press, 1978.

Brief biography and list of works.

B56   Hinson, Maurice. "12 x 11: Piano Music in Twentieth Century America." Chapel Hill, NC: Hinshaw Music, 1979.

Fifty nine pages of music, 31 cm., twelve selections by eleven composers. Contains Bassett's *Mobile.*

B57   Hunt, Paul B. "A Closer Look at the World Premiere of Leslie Bassett's Concerto Lirico for Trombone and Orchestra." *International Trombone Association Journal,* v.12, no.3, p.30-2, January 1984.

This lengthy three-page document celebrates Bassett's new work.

B58   "Inter American Music Festival, Seventh." [Review] by Irving Lowens. *High Fidelity and Musical America*, p.MA34,40, September 1976.

The Inter American Music Festival is held roughly every three years. Philadelphia Orchestra, Eugene Ormandy, conductor, performed *Echoes From an Invisible World* on May 19, 1976. Eight major concerts were scheduled over eight days during the Festival.

B59   *International Who's Who in Music and Musicians Directory*. 11th ed. Cambridge: Melrose Press Ltd., 1958.

Biography and list of compositions.

B60   Ivey, Ben. "Leslie Bassett -- A Biographical Profile." *International Trombone Association Newsletter,* v.6, no.3, p.2, April 1979.

A six-hundred word biography of Bassett accompanies the announcement that he is the guest of the Association's 1979 International Trombone Workshop, Peabody College, Nashville, TN, May 28-June 1, 1979, honoring him for his contribution to serious literature for the trombone. Faculty performed his *Sonata for Trombone and Piano, Suite for Unaccompanied Trombone, Quartet for Trombones,* and *Twelve Duos for Two or Four Trombones.*

B61   Johnson, Ellen Schultz. "An Interview with Leslie Bassett." 1983. [Interview, taped at the University of Kansas in Lawrence and typed]. 14 pages.

The one hour interview was typed and displayed in Thomas Gorton Music Library, Murphy Hall, site of the Symposium, for public use. Briefly the questions to which Bassett replied were: 1. At what age did you begin studying music? 2. Would you tell of some of your honors and experiences? 3. How do you characterize your music? 4. How do you compose? 5. What effect does the conductor have on your music? 6. For what level of students is your music suitable for performance? 7. What direction should young musicians who have skills in performing, composing, teaching try to go? 8. What do you consider the most satisfactory aspect of your career? 9. What is the effect of the growing trend of ensembles versus orchestras touring and performing on composing? 10. Do you have any comments on the copyright laws and their effect? 11. What do you do with your hand written manuscripts? 12. What are some of your experiences with festivals? 13. Would you say something about recordings of your compositions? Comments are included in this book.

B62   Johnson, Keith. "Salute to Cliff, Fanfare for Five Trumpets." *International Trumpet Guild Journal,* 10th Anniversary Edition, p.75, May 1986.

Suggested to the composer by Dennis L. Horton, trumpet teacher at Central Michigan University, this work was composed in honor of Clifford Lillya. Originally titled *Salute to Cliff,* it was premiered May 31, 1985 as an unpublicized addition to the final concert at the Albuquerque ITG Conference, prior to the surprise awarding of a commemorative plaque to Lillya from his former pupils.

B63   "Judges for 1989 Original Compositions Contest." *Triangle, Mu Phi Epsilon,* v.83, no.2, p.5, 1989.

Bassett participated.

B64   Kelley, Leslie B. "The Choral Music of Leslie Bassett." *Dissertation Abstracts,* V.37, 6130A-31A, April 1977.

This dissertation, Eastman School of Music, University of Rochester, contains biography, analysis, list of works, and other matters normally found in dissertations. It is available on microfilm.

B65   Kelley, Leslie B. "Choral Music of Leslie Bassett." *Choral Journal,* v.19, no.4, p.16-17, 1978.

Kelley comments on his doctoral research. Contains biography and list of works.

B66   Kerner, L. "Echoes From an Invisible World, Music: Various Views of Brahms and Barenhoim." *Village Voice,* v.24, p.65, March 5, 1979.

Review of New York Philharmonic concerts in February 1979, Zubin Metha, conductor, playing *Echoes From an Invisible World* for a Bicentennial celebration initiated by six orchestras, each commissioned one work and performed all six.

B67   Kiraly, P. "Retired but Relevant." *Symphony,* v.42, no.5, p.33, 1991.

Biography and portrait

B68   "Leslie Bassett and Don Jager Interviews." Voice of America Music Library Collection (Library of Congress). 1 sound tape reel, analog, 7 1/2 ips, double track, mono, 10 in.

Interview conducted by Nancy Lang of Voice of America.

B69   "Leslie Bassett." *American Music Teacher,* v.25, no.2, p.34, 1975.

Contains brief biography and portrait.

B70   Litton, James. (Westminster Choir College, Princeton, New Jersey) "Electronic Music in Church." *English Church Music,* p.23-8, 1972.

Criticism and a list of works including Bassett's work.

B71   "Liturgies, Organ." *Music Library Association Notes,* v. 42, no.4, p.856-7, 1986.

Review of Bassett's organ work, *Liturgies.*

B72   Londeix, Jean-Marie. " Sacred Music for saxophone." v.II. Cherry Hill, NJ: Roncorp, 1985.

Repertory of music and educational literature for saxophones.

B73   Lowens, Irving. "The Seventh International American Music Festival." *Hi Fi/Music America,* v.26, MA34+, September 1976.

Includes the performance of *Echoes from an Invisible World* at the Festival.

B74   Mackay, Andy. *Electronic Music.* Oxford: Phaidon, 1981. 124 pages.

Indispensible reading for the general reader. Invaluable glossary, index, colored illustrations, two columns per page. This 124 page book contains an excellent description of the origin and development of electronic music in terms that the non-scientific reader can understand. Contains portraits of fifty persons who influenced its development. Part 1: Instruments; Part 2: Music; Part 3: Musicians, including inventors, composers and performers and arranged alphabetically by surname.

B75   Mackey, Jocelyn. "Echoes From an Invisible World." *Pan Pipes, Sigma Alpha Iota,* p.2, Winter 1982.

Review of the recording of the Baltimore Symphony Orchestra, Sergiu Commissiona, conductor, produced by Composers Recordings, Inc. CRI SD 429. "This piece should appeal immediately to a large number of listeners; it is a composition which will yield new delights each time it is heard."

B76   McKenzie, Don. "Temperaments: Five Solos for Guitar." *Music Library Association Notes,* v.45, no.1, p.161-2, September 1988.

Review of *Temperaments*, written by Bassett, and *Shadows,* by William Albright, both guitar works.

B77   Mohler, John. "Soliloquies for B-flat Clarinet." *Clarinet,* p.40, Spring
       1979.

       Mohler comments on his performances of *Soliloquies.*

B78   Mortensen, Gary C. and Craig B. Parker. "The 1985 ITG Conference: A
       Synopsis, Final Concert." *International Trumpet Guild Journal,* v.10,
       no.1, p.46, September 1985.

       Excellent description of the premiere performance of *Salute to Cliff* at the
       Conference.

B79   "Music for Saxophone and Piano, Babbitt /Bassett /Smith /Wuorinin."
       Downbeat, v.45, no.1, p.28, 1977.

       A review of the recording of Bassett's *Music for Saxophone and Piano.*

B80   Myers, Kurtz. *Index to Record Reviews.* 5v. Boston: G. K. Hall, 1978.

       This index bases its material on recording reviews published in *Music
       Library Association Notes.*

B81   *New Grove Dictionary of American Music.* Edited by Wiley Hitchcock
       and Stanley Sadie. New York: Grove's Dictionary of Music, Inc., New
       York and London: Macmillan Press, Ltd, 1986. 4 volumes. v.1, p.159-160.

       This set contains a Biography of Bassett; Works: orchestral, chamber,
       choral, other works; Bibliography: contributed by D. Ewen, and A.
       Brown.

B82   *New Grove Dictionary of Music and Musicians.* Edited by Stanley Sadie.
       London: Macmillan Press, Ltd., 1980. 20 volumes.

       A comprehensive encyclopedia. The articles on Bassett and on Biagio
       Marini are written by Edith Boroff.

B83   New York Public Library, Library and Museum of the Performing Arts. *Dictionary Catalog of the Rodgers and Hammerstein Archives of Recorded Sound.* Boston: G. K. Hall, 1981. 15 volumes.

This is a catalog of the recordings owned by the library. Additional historical material owned by the library is not listed in this catalog, but is located at Lincoln Center in New York.

B84   New York Public Library, Research Libraries. *Dictionary Catalog of the Music Collection.* 2d ed., Boston: G. K. Hall, 1982. 32 volumes. Bassett: v.3, p.402.

The printed catalog of music owned by the library.

B85   "Nine Etudes in the Form of Duos." *Brass Bulletin,* no.12, p.58-61, 1975.

Reviews of Bassett's etudes for horn and piano appear here.

B86   *Pan Pipes, Sigma Alpha Iota Quarterly.*

Publishes an impressive winter issue, the only annual compilation of its kind in print and readily available to the public. Each year, for the immediate past year, it lists: premieres, performances, publications, recordings, news, and portraits of about 200 living American composers. Bassett appears here annually.

B87   Parks, Anne Florence. "Featured Concerts at the Ann Arbor Organ Conference." *Diapason,* v.72, p.26-7, April 1981.

Bassett's *Liturgies* is featured at this concert.

B88   Payne, A. "Festival of Moderns." *Music and Musicians,* v.14, p.61, December 1965.

A Review of Bassett's *Sonata for Horn.*

B89   "Pulitzer Prize, Some Winners in Music." *BMI Many Worlds of Music,* v.25, no.2, 1974.

Biography and portrait of Bassett.

B90   "Quintet for Brass Instruments, First Performance." *Brass Bulletin, International Magazine for Brass Players,* no. 68, p.[18], News Supplement 1989.

News.

B91   Rachleff, Larry. "An Interview with Leslie Bassett." *CBDNA Journal,* College Band Directors National Association, v.2, no.1, p.1-4, Winter 1985.

Excellent four-page interview.

B92   Rachleff, Larry. "Colors and Contours." *CBDNA Journal,* College Band Directors National Association, v.2, no.2, p.1-7, Winter 1986.

"In his single movement composition, Leslie Bassett continually infields and reworks his material, in a way that is similar to Baroque Fortspinning. The musical structure is based on a continual process of textural and gestural changes. Bassett's manipulation and varying developmental treatment of repeated concepts creates separate episodes and insures variety."

B93   *RILM, Abstracts of Music Literature, International Repertoire of Music Literature.* Published annually, 1968-current.

Lists references to Bassett's music.

B94   Rose, G. D. "Metamorphoses, Three Programs of Bassoon Music." *Dissertations Abstracts,* v. 52, 1939A, December 1991.

Doctoral dissertation discusses Bassett's music.

B95   Rosen, Jerome. "Trio for Violin, Clarinet, and Piano." *Music Library Association Notes,* v.46, p.822, March 1990.

Excellent critique of the music and the performance.

B96   Salzman, Eric. "Has the Avant-Garde Become the Establishment?" *Stereo Review,* v.37, p.100-1, August 1976.

This two-page discussion of Composers Recordings, Inc. philosophy on new issues of recordings contains interesting comments on the present state of the art of music. Salzman's comments end with " here are all the virtues and the defects of a do-good organization."

B97   Scanlon, R. "Leslie Bassett." *American Music Teacher,* v.25, no.2, p.34, 1975.

Contains brief biography and portrait.

B98   Scanlon, R. "Spotlight on Contemporary Composers: Leslie Bassett." *NATS Bulletin, National Association of Teachers of Singing,* xxxii/2, p.28-29, December 1975.

Contains short but comprehensive biographical sketch, composer's works for voice with accompaniment of either piano or instrumental ensemble, and a discussion.

B99   *Schwann Opus.* This publication is issued cumulative monthly and has special issues, such as classical, jazz, and performers.

A comprehensive record guide listing recordings currently available in retail music stores and giving composer's names, titles, performers, source and price.

B100 Scott, John. "Fantasy for Clarinet and Wind Ensemble." *The Clarinet,* p.50, May-June, 1988.

Review of this piece by Bassett for clarinet and wind ensemble.

B101 "Sextet for Piano and Strings, Has the Avant-garde Become the Establishment?" *Stereo Review,* v.37, p.100-1, August 1976.

This review of Bassett's *Sextet for Piano and Strings* contains comments on the present state of the art of music.

B102 Shuler, David. "Liturgies." *Music Library Association Notes,* v.42, no.4, p.856-8, June 1985.

Schuler discusses *Liturgies,* an organ work, in a lengthy review, giving quotes from Bassett's descriptive comments in the score and describing the music, written for and dedicated to Marilyn Mason.

B103 Sibley Music Library. *Catalog of Sound Recordings, University of Rochester, Eastman School of Music.* Boston: G. K. Hall, 1977. 14 v. Bassett: v.1, p.160.

Catalog of music owned by the library.

B104 Simmons, A. "Echoes From an Invisible World." *Music Journal,* v. 34, no.10, p.33, December 1976.

Simmons reviews the appeal and aesthetic intent of *Echoes from an Invisible World* crediting it with dreamlike images and imaginative and varied use of orchestral devices, which give it an immediate appeal, but suspects that the harmonic tension and indecisiveness of the overall aesthetic intent might suffer from repeated hearings. The review concludes that the conductor, Ormandy, highlighted the strengths of the work to the maximum effect.

B105   Skei, Allen B. "Time and Beyond, for Baritone Solo, Clarinet, Violoncello, and Piano." *Music Library Association Notes,* v.38, no.2, p.429-430, December 1981.

"Text from Emerson, Mark Van Doren, and Tagore. Freely chromatic, the settings, which last approximately nine minutes, generally project textures of elegant transparency absent of strong tonal centers."

B106   Smoley, L. M. "Music for Saxophone and Piano, Music in the Modern Manner." *American Record Guide,* v.41, p.49-51, December 1977.

A review of the recording featuring Bassett's *Music for Saxophone and Piano.*

B107   "Solo List for High School Trombones." *International Trombone Association Journal,* v.7, p.15, 1979.

Lists Bassett's *Sonata for Trombone and Piano* in its comprehensive list of solos suitable for high school trombonists.

B108   Stevens, Halsey. "Suite for Unaccompanied Trombone." *Music Library Association Notes,* v.27, no.1, p.154-5, September 1970.

Review of *Suite for Unaccompanied Trombone.*

B109   *Symphonic Catalog.* New York: Broadcast Music, Inc., 1971, Suppl. 1978.

Lists symphonic works available for purchase.

B110   Synnestveldt, Peter Nilen. "A Study of Three Contemporary Works for Orchestra." *Dissertation Abstracts,* v.48, 511A, September 1987.

This dissertation reviews Bassett's *Echoes From an Invisible World.*

B111   Thomas, J. "Illuminations, Potpouri." *Flutist Quarterly, National Flute Association,* v. 15, p.61, Summer 1990.

Review of Bassett's *Illuminations For Flute and Piano.*

B112   "Trio for Violin, Clarinet and Piano, Around the World in 180 Days With the Verdehr Trio." *Clarinet, International Clarinet Society,* v.10, no.2, p. 34, 1983.

Mentions the premiere of *Trio for Violin, Clarinet and Piano* at the University of Notre Dame by the Verdehr Trio, E. Ludwig-Verdehr.

B113   Tucker, W. E. "The Trombone Quartet, Its Appearance and Development Throughout History; and the Trombone Quartet in Chamber Music; Early Twentieth Century." *International Trombone Association Journal,* v.8, p.2, March 1980.

"Leslie Bassett composed and published a *Quartet for Trombones,* a one movement work of contrasting sections intended for use as a recital piece. The composer felt his composition embodies two contrasting aspects of trombone music: the rhythm and freedom of the jazz trombonist and the sense of dignity and sonority found in the works of such masters as the Gabrielis, Schutz and Monteverdi."

B114   Twardy, Chuck. "Leslie Bassett Asks--Why Is Music World Ossified?" *Lawrence Journal-World,* Sunday, March 13, 1983.

Excellent interview conducted during the Synposium of Contemporary Music, March 6-9, 1983, at the University of Kansas. Arts editor Twardy reports Bassett's comments on the state of contemporary music and its performance, why contemporary music symposia are necessary, speaking about concerts as an industry, selling a product, rather than exposing the public to the wealth of music, the language of composing, and some of Bassett's life experiences. About 1000 words.

A portrait of Bassett by Richard Gwin accompanies the interview.

B115 "Twelve Educational Institutions Receive NFMS-ASCAP Awards." *Music Clubs Magazine*, v.53, no.2, p.13, 1973.

News article describing artistic awards for outstanding performance or promotion of American music to participating institutions.

B116 "Two University of Michigan Professors Win Top Recognition." *School Musician*, v.46, p.27, November 1974.

News article describing an honor for Bassett.

B117 "Variations for Orchestra, Pulitzer Prize." *BMI Many Worlds of Music*, p.5, July 1966.

News report.

B118 Walker, B. H. "Recordings for the Clarinet and the Recording Artist." Augusta, GA: B. H. Walker, 1969.

A book for clarinetists which includes Bassett's work for clarinet.

B119 Weeks, Douglas Gilman. "A Review and Evaluation of Selected Contemporary Literature for Unaccompanied Trombone." *International Trombone Association Journal*, v.7, p.21-22, January 1979.

In his review of *Suite for Unaccompanied Trombone* Weeks writes, "The piece is atonal with each movement growing out of ideas stated at the beginning of the movement. Rhythmetically, it is a conservative work. Each movement has a meter of 4/4 which is felt throughout. There are no complex internal rhythmic structures. The full range of the trombone is utilized, from a pedal A to a D. The notes in between A and E are not used, thereby making an F attachment unnecessary."

"There are many wide leaps. Although there are many high notes, the tessitura lies within a comfortable middle range. The difficulty in performance is due to the endurance required, rather than technique. Because there is no accompaniment, there is no time to relax the embouchure. The techniques used are conventional and there is no unusual notation."

B120 *Who's Who in American Music.* Classical second edition. Edited by Jaques Cattell Press. New York: and London: R. R. Bowker, 1985. p. 38.

Contains Bassett's life, works, positions, awards, bibliography, memberships, and mailing address.

B121 Woodword, Henry. "Hear My Prayer, O Lord." *Music Library Association Notes,* v.25, no.3, p.607. March 1969.

Description of Bassett's *Hear My Prayer, O Lord* written for children's choir and orchestra.

B122 Wyatt, Lucius Reynolds. "The Mid-Twentieth-Century Orchestral Variation." 1953-1963." [Thesis]. Doctor of Philosophy, Department of Theory. Director: Dr. Robert V. Sutton, Eastman School of Music of the University of Rochester, NY, August, 1973. 448 pages. Microform available.

The thesis is an analysis and comparison of selected works by contemporary composers. Chapter 7, pages 176-213, is titled: *Variations for Orchestra*, by Leslie Bassett. The analysis is divided as follows: thematic materials, form, melodic style, harmony, tonality, rhythm and meter, and orchestration. Diagrams of formal structure of this work occupy pages 414-420.

B123 Wyatt, Lucius Reynolds. "Mid-Twentieth Century Orchestral Variations, 1953-1963." *Dissertation Abstracts,* v.34, p.7273A, May 1934.

Abstract of Wyatt's dissertation.

B124 Young, Charles Rochester. "Some Insights Into the Compositional Process of Leslie Bassett." *The Saxophone Symposium,* North American Saxophone Alliance, Alliance, v.15, no.3, p. 20-26, Summer 1990.

Consists of a biography, a question and answer interview, lists of selected works for band-wind ensemble, chamber music, unaccompanied instrumental solo, music for brass, and a selected discography.

Appendix A: Guest Composer Appearances

Leslie Bassett appeared as guest composer for performances of his works at festivals, symposia, etc. on the following dates, often giving talks.

American Symphony Orchestra League, Asilomar, CA 1959
Fresno State College, Fresno, CA 1966
East Carolina University, Greenville, NC 1967
Eastern Illinois University, Charleston, IL 1967
Interlochen Arts Academy, MI 1968
Indianapolis Symphony Orchestra, Indianapolis 1968
New England Conservatory of Music, Wind Ensemble Conference, Boston 1970
Central Missouri State College, Warrensburg 1971
Baldwin-Wallace College, Berea, OH 1971
Music Teachers Association of California 1971
Indiana University, Bloomington 1971
University of Maryland, College Park April 28, 1971
University of Delaware 1972
Interlochen Arts Academy, MI 1972
Western Michigan University, Convocation, Kalamozoo 1973
Kent State University, Kent, OH May 8, 1973
Berkshire Music Center, Tanglewood, Boston June-July 1973
Fresno State University, Fresno, CA March 15, 1974
Ball State University, Muncie, IN November 10, 1975
Kalamazoo College, Kalamazoo, MI April 8, 1976
Drake University, Des Moines, IA April 13-15, 1976
University of Wisconsin, River Falls May 3-5, 1976
University of Indiana, Bloomington November 18, 1976
Denison University, Granville, OH March 9, 1977
Oberlin Conservatory, Oberlin, OH March 18-19, 1977

Eastman School of Music, Rochester, NY November 10-11, 1977
Texas Tech University, Lubbock January 24-28, 1978
Bowling Green State Univ., Bowling Green, OH March 7, 1978
Peabody Conservatory of Music, Baltimore October 17-18, 1978
International Trombone Workshop, Peabody College, Nashville, TN
    January 30-31, 1979
Cork International Choral and Folk Dance Festival, Cork, Ireland April 25-29,
    1979
Baylor University, Waco, TX February 20-21, 1980
Southern Methodist University, Dallas, TX February 22, 1980
Boston University, Boston, MA March 14, 1980
San Jose State University, San Jose, CA October 1980
Chicago Music College, Roosevelt Univ. Chicago March 1981
University of Southern California, Los Angeles, CA April 1981
Memphis State University, Memphis, TN February 25-28, 1982
Bowling Green State Univ., Bowling Green, OH January 31, 1983
Florida State University, Tallahassee, FL February 24-26, 1983
University of Kansas, Lawrence, KS March 6-9, 1983
Kent State University, Kent, OH March 1-2, 1984
University of Colorado, Boulder, CO June 11-15, 1984
University of South Florida, Tampa, FL February 24-28, 1985
College Band Directors National Assoc, Boulder, CO March 1-2, 1985
Interlochen Arts Academy, MI March 15-16, 1985
Louisiana State University, LA February 26-March 2, 1986
Chamber Music Society of Baltimore, MD April 12-13, 1986
University of Southern California, Los Angelos,CA, Composer in residence
    February 1988
University of Redlands, Redlands, CA February 1988
Rockefeller Foundation Center, Villa Serbelloni, Italy April 1988
Grand Rapids Symphony, Grand Rapids, MI November 18-19, 1988
University of Wisconsin, Eau Claire, WI March 2-3, 1989
Crane School of Music, Potsdam College, State University of New York,
Potsdam February 6-7, 1989
Boston Share a Composer at Harvard, Northeastern, Tufts, Massachusetts,
Boston Universities, and Berkeley, CA March 12-17, 1990
Baldwin-Wallace College, Berea, OH April 25, 1990
International Trombone Workshop, Western Michigan University, Kalamazoo,
    MI June 1990

Appendix B: List of Publishers of Scores and Recordings

Abingdon Press, 201 East Eighth Ave., Nashville, TN 37206

Advance Recordings, European American Music Inc., P.O. Box, 850, Valley Forge, PA 19482.

American Composers Alliance, 170 W. 74th St., New York, NY 10023 (American Composers Edition Inc.)

Autograph Editions, New York, c/o Joseph Boonin Inc., 831 Main St., Hackensack, NJ 07601

Brass Press, 159 Eighth Ave. North, Nashville, TN, 37203

Franco Colombo Inc., 16 W. 61st St., New York, NY 10023

Composers Recordings Inc., (CRI) 73 Spring St. Room 506, New York, NY 10023

CPP/Belwin Inc., 15800 NW 48 Ave., Miami, FL 33014

Crystal Records, 2235 Willida Lane, Sedro Wooley, WA 98284

Desto Records, through CMS Records Inc., 4685 Manhattan, College Parkway, # 120 Bronx, New York, NY 10471

Galaxy Music Corp., 131 w. 86th St. New York, NY 10024.
Order music from E. C. Schirmer, Inc., 138 Ipswich St.
Boston, MA 02215

Golden Crest Records, P.O. Box 2859, Huntington Station, New York, NY 11746

Highgate Press (Galaxy)

Hinshaw Music Inc., P.O. Box 470, Chapel Hill, NC 27514.
Hinshaw piano music has been transferred to Alfred
Publishing Co., Inc. P.O. Box 10003, Van Nuys, CA
91410-0003

Robert King, 7 Canton St., North Easton, MA 02356

Leonarda Records, P.O. Box 1736, Cathedral Station, New York, NY 10025

Mark Educational Records Inc., 10815 Bodine Road, Clarence, NY 14031

Mel Bay Publications, P.O. Box 66, Pacific, MO 63069

Merion Music Inc., Theo Presser Co., Presser Place, Bryn Mawr, PA 19010

Musica Rara, 2 Great Marlborough Street, London, WI, England (Foreign Music Distributors, 13 Elleay Dr., Chester, NY 10918)

New World Records, 231 E. 51st St., New York, NY. 10036

C. F. Peters Corp., 373 Park Avenue South, New York, NY 10016

Philharmonia Co., 234 Fifth Avenue, 3rd Floor, New York, 10001

Prentice Hall Inc., 125 Sylvan Ave., Englewood Cliffs, NY. 07632

Theo Presser Co., Presser Place, Bryn Mawr, PA. 19010

Roseanne Music (Michael Lorimer), P.O. Box 833, Santa Barbara, CA 93102; Roseanne Music should be ordered from Mel Bay

University Music Press, c/o Hadcock Music House, P.O. Box 1267, Ann Arbor, MI 48106

World Library Publications, 3815 Willow Rd., P.O. Box 2701, Shiller Park, IL 60176

Appendix C: Alphabetical List of Titles

Codes prefixed by "W" refer to the items in the Classified List of Works; those by "D" to the Discography.

Almighty Eternal W47
Biagio Marini: Sonata for 2 bass Trombones
     and Continuo W73
Brass Quintet W7, W32
Brass Trio W8
Cantata, for City, Nation, World W48
Celebration in Praise of Earth W49, W84
Cello Duets W20
Clarinet Duets W21, D1
Collect (text: Leslie Bassett) W50, W77
Colloquy W85
Colors and Contours W1
Concerto da Camera for Trumpet and Chamber Ensemble W9, W22
Concerto for Orchestra W86
Concerto for Two Pianos and Orchestra W87, W98, D2
Concerto Grosso W2
Concerto Lirico for Trombone and Orchestra W10, W88
Configurations W99
Daniel Speer: Sonata and Gigue W76
Designs, Images and Textures W3, D3
Dialogues for Oboe and Piano W23, D4
Duo Concertante W24, D5
Duo-Inventions W25

Duos for Two or Four Trombones W11
Easter Triptych (text: Bible) W12, W66
Echoes from an Invisible World W89, D6
Ecologue, Ecomium and Evocation (Song of Songs) W51
Elaborations W100
A Family History W52
Fantasy for Clarinet and Wind Ensemble W4
Five Movements for Orchestra W90
Five Pieces for String Quartet W26
Forces W91
Four Songs W67
Four Statements W94
From a Source Evolving W92
Gio. Batt. Riccio: Three Canzonas W74
Gio. M. Cesare: La Hieronyma W75
Hear My Prayer, O Lord (Psalms 64) W53
Illuminations W27
Jade Garden, 4 Miniatures...Japanese and Chinese Poetry W68
The Lamb (text: Blake) W54
Liturgies (6 movements) W95
Lord, Who Hast Formed Me W55
Love Songs W69
Lullaby for Kirsten W5
A Masque of Bells W80
Mobile for Piano W101
Moon Canticle W56
Moonrise W57
Music for Cello and Piano W28, D7
Music for Four Horns W13
Music for Saxophone and Piano W29, D8, D9
Nonet W30
Notes in the Silence W58
Of Wind and Earth W59
Out of the Depths W60
Pierrot Songs W31, W70
Prayers for Divine Service (in Latin) W61
Preludes W102
Quartet for Trombones W14
Quintet for Piano and Strings W34, D10
Quintet for Strings W33
Remembrance W62

Appendix D: Chronological List of Works

Works are arranged by the date of composition.

1949 Quartet for Trombone W14
1950 String Quartet no. 1 [not published] W40
1951 Six Piano Pieces W103
     String Quartet no. 2 (not published) W41
1952 The Lamb W54
     Sonata for Horn and Piano W16
1953 Brass Trio W8
     Four Songs W67
     Toccata W96
     Trio for Viola, Clarinet and Piano W44, D16
1954 Quintet for Piano and Strings W34, D10
     Sonata for Trombone and Piano W17
1955 Clarinet Duets W21, D1
1956 Sonata for Viola and Piano W37
1957 Five Pieces for String Quartet W26
     Out of the Depths (de Profundis) W60
     Suite for Unaccompanied Trombone W18, W82, D14, D15
1958 Easter Triptych W12, W66
     Voluntaries W97
     Woodwind Quintet W19

1959 Cantata, for City, Nation, World W48
      Cello Duets W20
      Sonata for Violin and Piano W38
1960 Moonrise (text: Lawrence) W57
      Remembrance (text: Hoover Rupert) W62
1961 Five Movements for Orchestra W90
      Mobile for Piano W101
1962 Ecologue, Ecomium and Evocation (Song of Songs) W51
      Quintet for Piano and Strings W34, D10
      String Quartet, no. 3 W42
      To Music, Three Songs W72
1963 Variations for Orchestra W93, D18
1964 Designs, Images and Textures W3, D3
      Four Statements W94
1965 Hear My Prayer, O Lord (Psalms 64) W53
      Prayers for Divine Service (in Latin) W61
      Three Studies in Electronic Sound W78
1966 Elaborations W100
      Music for Cello and Piano W28, D7
      Notes in the Silence W58
      Triform W79
1967 Nonet W30
1968 Music for Saxophone and Piano W29, D8, D9
1969 Collect (text: Leslie Bassett) W50, W77
      Colloquy W85
      Moon Canticle W56
1970 Celebration, in Praise of Earth W49, W84
1971 Sextet for Piano and Strings W36, D11
1972 Forces W91
      Geo. M. Cesare: La Hieronyma W75
      Sounds Remembered W39, D13
1973 Biagio Marini: Sonata for 2 Bass Trombones and Continuo W73
      Notes in the Silence (text: Hammerskjold) W58
      Of Wind and Earth (text: Shelley, Bryant, St. Francis) W59
      Time and Beyond W71
1974 Duos for Two or Four Trombones (twelve) W11
      Music for Four Horns W13
1975 Echoes from an Invisible World W89, D6
      Love Songs W69
      Wind Music W46

1976 Concerto for Two Pianos and Orchestra W87, W98, D12
     Soliloquies W82, D12
1977 Jade Garden, 4 miniatures...Japanese and Chinese poetry W68
     Sounds, Shapes and Symbols W6
1978 String Quartet, no. 4 W43
1979 Daniel Speer: Sonata and Gigue W76
     Gio. Batt. Riccio: Three Canzonas W74
     A Ring of Emeralds W63
     Sextet for Flutes, Clarinets and Strings W35
     Temperaments, Five W83
1980 A Masque of Bells W80
     Liturgies (six movements) W95
     Trio for Violin, Clarinet and Piano W45, D17
1981 A Family History (text: Leslie Bassett) W52
     Concerto da Camera for Trumpet and Chamber Ensemble W9, W22
     Lord, Who Hast Formed Me (anthem text: George Herbert) W55
     Sing to the Lord (Psalms 95) W64
1982 Concerto Grosso W2
1983 Concerto Lirico for Trombone and Orchestra W10, W88
1984 Colors and Contours W1
     Duo Concertante D5, W24
     Preludes (seven) W102
1985 From a Source Evolving W92
     Lullaby for Kirsten W5
     Salute to Cliff W15
1986 Fantasy for Clarinet and Wind Ensemble W4
1987 Whoe'er She Be W65
     Dialogues for Oboe and Piano W23, D4
1988 Brass Quintet W7, W32
     Configurations W99
     Duo-Inventions W25
     Pierrot Songs (text: Giraud, German by Hartleben) W31, W70
1989 Almighty, Eternal W47
     Iluminations for Flute and Piano W27
1991 Concerto for Orchestra W86

Persons Index

General Index

ADDENDA: PUBLICATIONS

Arias. Clarinet and piano. 12 minutes. Peters, c1993. Commissioned by the International Clarinet Association; premiere performance by Fred Ormand at the Association's 1993 Conference in Belgium.

Metamorphoses. Bassoon solo. 15 minutes. Peters, c1992. Each of the eight *Metamorphoses* emerges and unfolds from a brief source, a fragment drawn from orchestral bassoon literature. The sources are: Stravinsky: *The Rite of Spring,* Prokofiev: *Peter and the Wolf,* Tchaikovsky: *Symphony No. 4,* Beethoven: *Symphonies No. 3, 1 and 8,* Scriabin: *Poem of Ecstacy,* Chabrier: *Espana. Metamorphoses* was commissioned by friends, colleagues and students of L. Hugh Cooper, Professor of Music (Bassoon) at the University of Michigan, on the occasion of his retirement and in appreciation of his many contributions to performance, teaching and research. The premiere performance was by Gwendolyn (Wendy) Rose at the University on February 12, 1991, with immediate subsequent performances by Richard Beene.

ADDENDA: RECENT PERFORMANCES

From a Source Evolving

American Composers Orchestra, conducted by Lawrence Leighton Smith, at Carnegie Hall, New York, October 13, 1991.

Illuminations for Flute and Piano

Bryan-Keys Duo, International Flute Congress, New York, August 13, 1991.

Colors and Contours

Many performances, at such places as Miami University, Oxford, OH, April 21, 1992; Long Beach State University, Long Beach, CA, May 15, 1992; Interlochen Center for the Arts, Interlochen, MI, July 8, 1992.

About the Author

ELLEN S. JOHNSON is a retired music librarian and researcher. She has published in professional journals and has lectured on archival music collections and music copyright.